Laughter~Silvered
Wings

Remembering
the Air Force II

Laughter~Silvered
Wings

Remembering
the Air Force II

J. Douglas Harvey

McClelland and Stewart

The Canadian Publishers
McClelland and Stewart Limited
25 Hollinger Road
Toronto, M4B 3G2

Canadian Cataloguing in Publication Data

Harvey, J. Douglas, 1922-
  Laughter-silvered wings

ISBN 0-7710-4045-8

1. Harvey, J. Douglas, 1922-   2. Canada. Royal
Canadian Air Force – Biography.   3. Canada. Royal
Canadian Air Force – Anecdotes, facetiae, satire,
etc. I. Title.

UG635.C2H37 1984   358.4´00971   C84-098892-3

Printed and bound in Canada

For Helen

Other Books by J. Douglas Harvey

Boys, Bombs, and Brussels Sprouts (1981)
The Tumbling Mirth: Remembering the Air Force (1983)

Contents

Introduction

I had no intention of writing this book, thinking I had already contributed all I could to the subject in *The Tumbling Mirth: Remembering the Air Force*. But so many people have continued to contact me offering their own hilarious stories, that I couldn't resist passing them on to you.

Like *The Tumbling Mirth* – and like *Boys, Bombs, and Brussels Sprouts* – this book has been written to show the spirit that encompassed all aspects of the Royal Canadian Air Force. Spirit was the one thing that made that magnificent service supreme and, of course, it's the missing ingredient in Canada's present unified charade.

There are false prophets loose in Canada who will tell you that a country's military can be analyzed, standardized, computerized, packaged, and labelled. You should take particular care to examine the military credentials of these advocates of a unified, military automation. You'll find that unification is only a Canadian fantasy. (Luckily, it is not a NATO problem!)

It has been twenty years since the unifying process began in Canada. Surely that is time enough to recognize that the experiment has proved a dismal failure. Surely we have learned that a spiritless bunch of people, no matter how well-intentioned, cannot provide the first-class arms this country deserves.

A first-class military service lives on spirit, excels on spirit, and succeeds on spirit. It is the very essence of victory. Anything that smothers that spirit does irreparable damage, for it destroys the military's will to accept unacceptable odds.

If we Canadians feel that our country is worth defending in this uncertain world, we should make sure our military have that one essential. All the money, all the rank, and all the creature comforts can't buy spirit. It may be difficult to define but it is free.

For those who may have difficulty defining spirit, the anecdotes and yarns in this book will help. They are from an era when Canada had a service called the Royal Canadian Air Force – and brother, it had spirit!

I have only been allowed to list some of the people who contributed stories. Others did not wish their names to appear. While I understand their reluctance, I do regret their decision. But to all I say thank you for sharing the fun.

J.D.H.

Contributors

• Shirley (Wilson) Allen, Norman Avery • Dorothy (Calder) Beale, Marguerite (Bergeron) Belisle, Gord Bell, Shirley (Edwards) Blais, Edna (Moore) Blakely, Marion C. Boyle, Eleanor K. Browne, Harry Bryant • Beth (Stevenson) Carson, John Clare, Butch Cleaver, Patricia (Hall) Clifford, Ed Clinton, Chris Cooke • T.G.M. Davidson, Davie Davis, Elsie Duncan, Frances (Burke) Dutton • Joan (Davis) Ellis • Elizabeth Falcone, Eunice Kay (Godfrey) Falcone, Alison (Duncan) Ferris, Jean "Johnny" Fontaine, Tommie C. Frey • Ernie Gent, John E. Goldsmith, Suzette (Comeau) Gregoire • Eileen (Scott) Hall, Mary (Baird) Harland, Elizabeth (Kennedy) Harrison, Beatrice L. Henning, Amy Hollister, Barbara (Barry) Howard • "Peewee" Armstrong Jones, Bob Jordan • Pearl King, Marjorie (Oliver) Kirkland, W. Kynaston • Len Lapeer, G.V. Lloyd, J.D. Long, Maurice Longfield, Jim Lovelace • Kathleen (Berry) MacDonald, Lyall MacLeod, Isabel (Anderson) MacPhail, Veronica Mair, Helen (Hall) Marellus, Veronica (Haysom) Marr, Eleanor Martin, Aussie Maxwell, Arch McDonald, Mary (King) McDonald, Joan (Williams) McDowell, Phoebe (Ward) McLeod, Kathleen (Ritchie) McNeil, Peggy A. Millar, A.E. "Muff" Mills, Christine (Cooke) Murphy, Gladys (Rainey) Musselman • Anna M. (Monroe) Nadeau, Betty (Kiddle) Neilson, Eric Nicol • Ruth (Moores) O'Brien • Chas E. Pearson, George Penfold, Mildred C. Perrin • Rita (Sullivan) Quinn • Gwennyth (Bradley) Randolph, Jeanne Richard, Keith Roberts, Tom Robinson, H.W. Rourke, Jean (Umehara) Ruse • Frank Scholfield, M. Sikes, Al Spencer • Joyce (Williams) Teague, Joyce Teal, Jim "Sea Level" Thompson, Ruth (Rogers) Thompson, Dave Thorne, Derrick Todd, Celea Toomik • Jessie (Johnson) Waterman, Frank Weiser, Jack Western, Kathleen (Scott) Williams, Margaret Williams, Jean (Carson) Wills, Dorothy (Stuart) Wilson, Roy Wood, John H. Woodrow, Barbara (Neale) Wright

And a special thanks to Tom Farley, who has allowed the use of three of his poems previously published in *It Was A Plane* (Ryerson Press).

Cartoons by Ray Tracey

Oh, I have slipped the surly bonds of earth
And danced the skies on laughter-silvered wings . . . .

FROM "HIGH FLIGHT"
JOHN GILLESPIE MAGEE, JUNIOR

In the summer of 1941 I went to Niagara Camp for two weeks with the Non-Permanent Army Militia Sault Ste. Marie/Sudbury (machine gun) Regiment. Due to an assignment to help carry out National Registration – which required a non-commissioned officer to perform – I was promoted to Corporal after only three weeks service!

During instruction (wearing World War One uniforms) we were trained on the Boys' anti-tank rifle. It had two sight settings: 300 yards and 500 yards. Having read in *Time* magazine that German Panzer tanks had .50 calibre machine guns effective at 2,000 yards, I asked the drill Sergeant: "How do you attack a German tank with this weapon?"

The answer was: "Hold your fire until it comes into range, and then fire at the slits."

Very shortly thereafter I joined the air force.

* * *

I have often asked myself why I enlisted in the RCAF. I was much older than most of the airwomen I served with. I suppose I had wearied of the drab business world of keeping books and decided a change of scene would be good for me . . . .

I also wanted to be a significant part of Canada's war effort, and contribute something to the women's cause. This was an opportunity for Canadian women to prove themselves equal to Russian women. We *did* prove that we were more than a decorative addition to the population – and I like to feel that we spearheaded the Women's Movement, despite the criticism slung at our generation today.

Struts and Castor Oil

In 1918 I did my flying training at Camp Borden on JN-4's, the old Curtis Jenny aircraft. They were quite the machine. The cockpit bristled with three flight instruments: a petrol gauge, an oil gauge, and a rev counter.

One or two of the aircraft did have airspeed indicators fastened on an outer strut. This was a spring-loaded piece of metal that was pushed back by the airstream and was calibrated in miles-per-hour. (A good aircraft could get sixty-five miles-per-hour flat out. We landed at forty-five miles-per-hour.) Another couple of aircraft were also fitted with a compass for reconnaissance flights; and one had a bomb sight for camera-obscura bombing training.

One Sunday morning I was airborne with an instructor on dual training. I had about three hours in my log book and we were practising approaches in a farmer's field, near New Lowell. As we came in for our approach I spotted an open touring car parked on a nearby road. It was full of girls, and they were waving at us.

It was while I was turned around in the cockpit waving back that the aircraft hit a tree. The instructor grabbed the controls – but it was too late. The Jenny stalled out and fell into a ravine. When I released my harness I fell into a small brook, and the only injury I received was a split lip. Except for a cut on his knee the instructor was okay, too.

At daybreak the next morning I was sleeping soundly in my tent when I got a rap on the shoulder. It was my instructor, following the laid-down rule: *After a crash get airborne again as quickly as possible – before you lose your nerve.*

"Come on!" he cried. "We're going flying!"

*   *   *

Castor oil was the number one ingredient of the rotary engines used in the early flying days. Spewed out of the exhaust ports at a great rate it covered everything – including the pilots in their open cockpits.

No one ever suffered from constipation when flying a rotary-engined aircraft. The fumes from the oil splashing over the cockpit took care of that little matter.

*   *   *

In the early days of the RCAF, non-commissioned officers didn't put a man on charge unless he had committed a major crime. If they did it was considered a bad reflection on their ability to handle men. In those days they were all given a fairly wide latitude in handing out punishments.

Washing down aircraft was a particular favourite. It was one hell of a job because all the early aircraft had rotary engines that flung oil in all directions. The oil simply spewed out of the exhaust ports since there was no oil-return to the sump. Every aircraft had to be washed down and scraped at the end of each day's flying.

I know – from hard experience – that you used a dull putty knife and a solution of Okite and water. This was a form of caustic soda which really ate the skin off your fingers. All the aircraft were fabric-covered – and woe to the airman who stuck his knife through the fabric! He then had to spend all of his free time massaging the grounds around the barracks.

* * *

When I first arrived at RCAF Station Camp Borden in the 1920s it was sometimes pretty tough going. The name of the game was discipline. The base was run by the Sergeant Major and it seemed that everyone from the CO down deferred to him. He was the most renowned Senior Warrant Officer the RCAF ever had, and his name was Jimmy Dyte.

Dyte was a real stickler for everything air force – but in his own way he was a fine gentleman and a friend in need to any deserving airman. He had his own unique and ingenious ways of impressing service regulations on lowly recruits. I remember one in particular . . . .

In those days, airmen in "walking-out uniform" were obliged to carry a swagger stick. This was a neat little wooden article about two feet long. It was painted black and had a silver-coloured head embossed with the air force crest.

You were to carry this stick in the right hand, swinging it to and fro parallel to the ground as you marched along. The only exception was when approaching an officer, when it was to be placed smartly under the left armpit in time with your footsteps. You went through a complicated series of manoeuvres to produce a

17

smart salute – then reversed the procedure (always remembering to keep time) after saluting.

Whenever an airman failed to salute in the prescribed manner he was immediately turned over to Jimmy Dyte for appropriate action. Dyte would promptly march the culprit to the greenhouse, a building which was about twelve windows high from foundation to roof, and perhaps 100 windows long. There, he would position the airman about six feet away from the left corner of the greenhouse. On command, the airman would take two paces forward, place his swagger stick in the appropriate position for saluting, salute, take two paces to the rear, return his stick to the marching position, and repeat the process until he had saluted each window in the vertical row.

Having done this he was moved one pace to the right, facing another vertical row . . . . And this kept up until each and every window in the greenhouse – all 1,200 of them – had been correctly saluted. I always figured the punishment was as hard on Dyte as it was on the airman. He was the one who had to stand there and ensure that each salute was made according to regulations.

* * *

Camp Borden in the 1920s and 1930s was one large sand dune. The majority of the roads leading to the small country towns were sand tracks. You travelled to places like Brentwood, Angus, New Lowell, or Creemore over and on (and sometimes in) sand.

Sundays on camp were dead periods. Victorian dead. Nothing was permitted and just for something to do many airmen would take walks along the sand roads. Three of us were walking the roads one hot Sunday morning. We were enroute back to camp when a large Cadillac touring car came bouncing along and stopped beside us.

The car was a 1917 model and it was driven by a hard rock Squadron Leader who was a legend in his time. As lowly airmen we wanted no part of this guy – but when the dust had settled he barked, in a voice only a mother could love: "Get in!"

"No thanks, sir," one of us replied. "We're just out for our morning constitutional."

"Get in!" rasped the voice. "I didn't stop for nothing."

Whereupon we dutifully climbed into the back seat – which in those ancient cars placed you higher than the front seat, so that you sort of looked down into the cockpit. With a grinding of gears we got underway, and one of my buddies leaned forward to make conversation. "Nice weather we're having, sir."

To which the voice growled, "Like hell it is! It's too goddamn dry."

Stopping in the sand was penance enough for the Squadron Leader. He wasn't about to converse with lowly airmen – even if he had insisted that they take a Sunday drive.

*   *   *

When the first RCAF Instrument Flying Course was held at Camp Borden in the winter of 1931-32, a number of bush pilots were invited to take part. Upon admission to the course they were placed on the RCAF Reserve List and obliged to wear uniforms. Which led to some amusing incidents.

I chummed with one of the bush pilots, who happened to personify everything you've ever heard of that rugged and enterprising breed of airmen. A huge hunk of man, he was the ugliest looking person I ever saw – and the nicest person I would want to meet.

Two of the instructors were also extremely homely: a real match for my bush pilot friend. Both of them were Flight Lieutenants who had received their scarred and hatched looks from landing the old Avro 504's on their noses instead of their wheels. They were just plain ugly to look at.

One day, as my friend and I were walking up the hangar line, the two Flight Lieutenants approached us from an acute angle. Ever conscious of the strict regulations existing at Camp Borden, I whipped up a fast salute. My friend didn't bother.

One hell of a roar erupted from the two officers. They demanded that my friend halt and salute them. Approaching, he gave his salute; and then he looked them over very carefully. Finally, with a smile, he said: "I must be the third member of your ugly buggers club."

He got seven days Orderly Officer duty for that remark.

*   *   *

We were stationed at Camp Borden in the Dirty Thirties, and visiting Shea's Vaudeville Theatre was the "in" thing to do. We lived for the weekends and the chance to get down to Toronto for the show. It gave us something to talk about the following week – just as television does for its audiences today. Except that we weren't jaded from over-exposure. Just the opposite. We sat spellbound through each and every act.

One Monday after work we had, as usual, repaired to the Sergeants' Mess for a few pints. The air was filled with descriptions of the various acts and star performers at Shea's on the previous Saturday. I was sitting next to three senior NCO's, none of whom was noted for a command of the language.

One of them, a Warrant Officer, was describing the acts he had liked best. "I'll tell you, Bill," he said to his fellow Warrant Officer, "there was a girl playing a harp. She was the best goddamn harpoonist I've ever heard!"

At this point the third NCO, who was a Flight Sergeant, noticed that the speaker was wearing new glasses. He remarked on how sharp they looked, then asked if they were issue or if the Warrant Officer had bought them. When he found out that they had been purchased, the Flight Sergeant announced: "By God, I need new glasses – and I sure like yours. Can you give me the name of your optimist?"

Needle, Ball, Airspeed

After some careful thought I decided that my student pilot was ready to solo. He could handle the twin-engined Anson with a confidence I found rare among my students. At the time I made my decision we were airborne and approaching the field to join the circuit. *After we land I'll send him solo*, I thought. *With his confidence everything should be okay.*

With the student at the controls we joined the circuit and proceeded into the landing pattern. It was lunch time, and it seemed that every aircraft in Canada was in our circuit. It had extended miles downwind as novice pilots tried to keep some separation from aircraft ahead of them and yet avoid overshooting. A real rat race.

My student appeared to be judging his distance fairly well. We were following a staggering line of descending Ansons, some touching down, others pulling up and going around. In such circumstances, it was my practice to avoid talking too much, in case it destroyed the student's confidence. But suddenly we were too low and too close to the aircraft immediately in front of us.

"More power!" I yelled.

The student jammed both throttles ahead and the engines roared.

"Overshoot!" I ordered. "You're too close to that guy." But just as I said this the Anson in front of us began to overshoot. "Okay. You're okay now," I said. "He's overshooting."

The student yanked off the power and pulled the wheels up in almost one motion.

"Full power!" I screamed, frantically grabbing for the controls.

Too late! We bounced crazily on one partially raised wheel and careened onto the infield grass, headed for the hangar. The props began chewing into the ground – there was a hell of a banging and scraping – one wing tip dug in and swung us around . . . . When the dust settled we were almost exactly in our original parking spot on the edge of the tarmac. But what a mess.

I sat there, completely stunned, wondering how in *hell*, just a few minutes earlier, I had been so sure my student was ready for solo. He was the one leading the way as we struggled to the rear door, and he was the one who grasped the door handle.

The door fell out on the tarmac.

Stepping through the opening, the student turned to me. "That door," he said calmly, "will have to be repaired."

Confidence.

*   *   *

One of the wartime posters seen everywhere depicted RCAF aircraft in various attitudes of flight. Underneath a slogan read: *Keep 'em Flying*. This slogan was quickly adopted and you heard it everywhere.

At one period during the war I was a flying instructor on Tiger Moths at Pendleton, and on my birthday I was testing a brand new Tiger. Shortly after takeoff the controls froze and I had to bail out. I landed unhurt but I was a little worried. I had just bent a brand new aircraft.

Later that day, when I picked up my mail from the Mess, there was a birthday card from my Dad. *Happy Birthday, Son*, it read. *Keep 'em Flying*.

*   *   *

I was nearing the end of my elementary flying training in May of 1943. After completing a tour of operations over Germany as an observer – and after spending a year on the ground at Trenton arguing for a pilot's course – I was finally getting along towards the coveted Wings.

Three of us were selected for night flying, and it was with some trepidation that we wobbled out to the mighty Tiger Moths accompanied by instructors other than our own. My new instructor was a mature Flying Officer who normally gave twenty-hour check rides. The two of us did a walk-around with flashlights, climbed in, buckled up, got her started, and taxied out to the runway.

First, the instructor took off, did a circuit, and landed. Next, he handed over to me to taxi and follow him through on the controls while he did a takeoff and landing. That dual landing would have done credit to a scared kangaroo; but *after* that – when the next two circuits were left strictly up to me – the landings resembled controlled crashes. Finally, we taxied back to the takeoff point, and I looked around to see that my mentor was leaving.

"Are we all through?" I asked.

"You're not," he said. "You're on your own. Do two more circuits. I'm leaving because there's no use in both of us getting killed. If you get back I'll see you in the Mess and buy you a drink. You'll need it!"

* * *

We were at No. 6 Elementary Flying Training Station, Prince Albert, Saskatchewan – and it was after we all had about thirty flying hours that we decided we should do some combat flying. Two of us would make plans to meet after takeoff and we would take turns chasing one another about the sky.

One day, I and a fellow named MacDonald were busy chasing around. I was flying right behind him, following right on his tail, when his plane went nearly straight up. I did the same thing – and happened to glance over my shoulder in time to see a steel cable pass just below my Tiger Moth. After we landed we figured out that it was a cable stretched across the North Saskatchewan River to be used by the ferry . . . . The incident took all thoughts of playing war games right out of our minds.

* * *

In December 1942, on completion of Initial Training School, I was selected to be sent on for an observer's course rather than the pilot's training I wanted. Although I was disappointed I could hardly object after scoring the lowest marks ever achieved in a Link Trainer.

Forthwith I reported to No. 1 Bombing and Gunnery School at Jarvis, Ontario. Here I discovered that I would be challenging the skies in the mighty Anson and Bolingbroke "bombers." The Boley, I found, had been equipped with Fraser-Nash gun turrets designed, no doubt, for a breed of Singer Midgets and not 200-pound Canadians in bulky flying suits. Nevertheless we began range firing over Lake Erie using target-drogues towed by Lysander aircraft.

My inability to lead a moving target nicely matched my perfect score of zero hits on the skeet range – as I had anticipated it might. None of which worried me until I discovered that I had to score at least 4 per cent hits in order to graduate from the course. I began to think that I would spend the rest of my days at No. 1 B&G.

Fortunately (due to a series of near miraculous passes in a barrack's crap game) I was able to purchase a forty-ouncer of rye whiskey. Suitably armed, I repaired to the drogue pilot's room where I explained my predicament to an understanding pilot. He became even more understanding after the presentation of my humble offering. He agreed to see what might be done.

Lo and behold! On my very next flight the Lysander pilot towing the drogue drew alongside our Bolingbroke, waving his hand in friendly greeting. As he flew ahead, the drogue on its long steel cable began drifting back. When it was directly opposite and hardly off our wing tip I merrily emptied my belt of ammunition into it. No leading required. A straight on, twenty-foot shot.

When the markers counted up the hits I had scored an impressive 9 per cent. Now I could go about winning the war. Piece of cake.

*   *   *

I was training for my pilot's Wings late in 1944, when the need for aircrew was rapidly diminishing – and I was extremely nervous about being washed-out. The final few weeks were nerve-wracking. Any goof, no matter how minor, took on major proportions. Twelve students bit the dust with just two weeks to go.

My last few flying hours were logged at Granum, a relief field just a few miles north of our No. 7 Service Flying Training School at Macleod, Alberta. Granum, like all satellite fields, hadn't any permanent facilities: just a triangle of asphalt runways that served both as runways and taxi strips. Flying Control was provided from a truck parked at the end of the runway in use, and consisted of a guy holding an Aldis lamp. A green light meant that it was okay to take off or land. A red light meant the reverse. In an emergency, a red flare would be fired off (usually because a student was trying to land with his wheels up) and a white flare meant that all flying was washed out for the day.

I was doing circuits and bumps in an old Mark II Anson. It was a gorgeous October day and I was taxiing along to the takeoff point, the twin-engined Anson purring along, the sun streaming into the cockpit. Suddenly, I spotted a gopher standing directly in front of my aircraft. It was on its hind legs in the characteristic pose of all gophers: arms hanging down over a fat, round belly, teeth sticking out. *You'd better move, gopher, or you'll get run over*, I thought, as the Anson bore down on it.

The Anson's wheels had a track of some eight feet, so I was sure I could straddle the gopher and avoid hitting it. I leaned forward into the windscreen as I approached, keeping the gopher in sight as long as possible. I was hoping the little guy would stay put, but the engines must have frightened it. At the last second it ran under my port wheel.

Braking to a stop I leaned out of my cockpit and saw the gopher lying on its side, twitching and kicking. What to do? If I got out to help I'd be reported. If I tried to turn the Anson around I'd be reported. In either case – there would go the coveted Wings . . . .

But I knew I couldn't leave the little thing to suffer. Getting the green light to move out for takeoff I gunned the Anson down the runway, then cut the throttle and turned off. Takeoff aborted, I began taxiing back, looking for the gopher; and when I found it, still twitching at the side of the runway, I took careful aim with the port tire and put it out of its misery.

I'm glad I did it. I'm also glad that I still got my Wings.

* * *

Things were often frantic in the early days of the war at No. I Manning Depot. Overseas Headquarters was screaming for radio technicians, and recruiting officers across Canada were signing up anyone who was a radio ham.

I was given thirty days to bring these raw recruits up to standard and send them on their way to Halifax, where they'd catch a boat for England. Things moved fast and often – but on the evening before the course left, when everyone gathered in the Wet canteen to celebrate, I asked permission to join them for a farewell drink.

I only stayed for about fifteen minutes; and I was just getting up to go when a very large chap slapped me on the back – a slap that I could feel right down to my toes. When I turned around the man looked me straight in the eye. "Sir, you are one miserable son-of-a-bitch," he said. "But I love you just the same."

* * *

When 408 Squadron began flying Lancasters at Rockcliffe airbase in 1948, pilots on the other squadrons at Rockcliffe wanted to get checked out on them. They badgered every pilot for a ride.

One aggressive Squadron Leader was able to throw his rank around and demand a flight. He was a Flight Commander on a

sister squadron flying Canso aircraft, and he desperately wanted to have some four-engine time in his logbook. For the occasion, I acted as his flight engineer – and this guy was so terrible it was unbelievable. On each landing we bounced higher and harder. He hit so hard on one landing that my headset bounced off my head!

To make matters worse, the old Lancs only had one proper pilot's seat and one set of controls. When dual instruction was being given, the check pilot rode on the engineer's jump seat. Although the control columns were yoked together the check pilot didn't have brakes on his side . . . . In addition, it happened to be winter.

We were using the shortest of the runways – one that led into the RCMP hangar and after that a large hill. After smashing the Lanc to the runway the Squadron Leader over-steered, and the check pilot was helpless to stop the wildly skidding Lancaster. Before we knew it we were buried deep in a large snowbank.

The Squadron Leader turned to me, where I stood behind both pilots. "Okay," he barked. "Dig us out."

I turned to the check pilot for confirmation – just in time to hear him say: "He's not bad. He's not even terrible. He's fucking atrocious!"

* * *

At Rockcliffe airbase in 1948 we had one B-25 Mitchell aircraft. I think it was the only one in eastern Canada at that time. One day, Denny de Niverville, one of the RCAF's keenest pilots, took off in the Mitchell for some local training. His co-pilot was the RAF exchange pilot, Pete Farrow.

When they had completed their training exercises and were returning to base, Denny decided to see if he could do a slow roll in the medium bomber. The mistake he made was trying it over Ottawa, where a Squadron Leader saw the roll and reported the incident.

At the Board of Inquiry, Denny adopted a "I wouldn't ever do that sort of thing – it's unauthorized" attitude. So the star witness, the RAF pilot, was called; and the question was put to him: "Did the Mitchell bomber in which you were flying do a slow roll?"

The RAF bloke said that since he was newly arrived in Canada and so unused to Canadian airspace, he had been studying his

Canada Air Pilot book for much of the flight and wasn't the least certain just what manoeuvres the captain had performed.

Case dismissed for lack of evidence.

* * *

In the early 1940s, No. 31 General Reconnaissance Navigation School at Charlottetown, Prince Edward Island, was equipped with Mark I Ansons as well as a substantial number of Mark II's. The main difference between these airplanes was in engine type and airframe construction. The Mark I was a metal and fabric product powered by Cheetah-9 engines, while the Mark II was almost entirely plywood and had Jacobs engines. Performance of the two craft was comparable, except when a forced landing or a crash occurred. Then the Mark I tended to remain around to help explain what happened. The Mark II was generally converted into a pile of cables, pipes, and toothpicks.

Each morning every staff pilot would consult the Flight Program Board to ascertain his aircraft, students, and type of trip. He might be allotted either a Mark I or Mark II. To most people this was immaterial – but I somehow feel that on one particular morning Lady Luck intervened, and as a result I am still around.

As a staff wireless operator I usually flew with the same pilot: a stocky, jovial Sergeant named Arthur. Arthur lived to fly and looked forward to the day when he would fly Mosquitoes or Beaufighters in a place where his exceptional talents would be appreciated. In the meantime he piled up flying hours, gained experience, and at every opportunity beat up most of PEI with his low flying.

This morning we were detailed to fly a Mark I, and our trip covered a route rather popular with Arthur. After proceeding to several dead-reckoning positions over the Gulf of St. Lawrence and making a landfall at East Point, PEI, we would descend gradually to 300 feet while flying along the south coast towards Souris. At Souris there would be a turn into the bay and a gentle climb so that our student navigators might photograph the harbour before returning to base.

The reason Arthur particularly enjoyed this outing was because he had the chance to do some low flying that would scare hell out of the natives as well as his crew. In other words: when Arthur reached East Point he went bananas. Skimming over the waves he

would swing into Souris harbour at high speed, apply maximum power, and climb steeply as the unfortunate navigators struggled with their heavy camera. Directly over the town he would cut power, roll the old crate over, and dive for a tree-covered point, only recovering at the last moment. I had been on this suicide mission many times before – but this morning I not only could hear organ music, I could smell flowers. The navigators had abandoned their camera long since. The stage was set for Arthur's finale . . . .

We fell from the sky like a rock, loose items floating around our heads. During the pull-out we were suddenly forced to the floor, and at the same time there was a sickening shudder. Only trees were visible outside – and although, in an attempt to climb, Arthur drove the throttles through the gate for maximum power, there was a thunderous bang before we gained sufficient height to break clear. In a matter of seconds the floor was covered with spruce boughs. A branch six feet long and one inch thick rested on a ledge after passing Arthur's left ear on the way in!

It was several minutes before sufficient height was acquired and some degree of stability maintained. Fighting a vicious wind (there was no longer a windscreen) I made my way up front and viewed the carnage with amazement. The main problem at this point was a lack of forward visibility caused by spruce foliage lodged in the aircraft's crushed nose. An effort was made to reach outside and break off small twigs, and this helped a little. Fortunately, Arthur was one of the few pilots who carried goggles. The spruce boughs were blowing inside and the rest of his face began to take on the appearance of raw hamburger from the needles.

During the twenty minute flight to Charlottetown there began to be control problems as well. The use of the elevators tended to turn the aircraft to port and cause loss of height at the same time. Our approach to the field was long and cautious and Arthur managed an excellent landing. Once on the ground we must have looked as though a wrecker's yard had sprouted wings. By the time we reached our hangar the only thing missing was the station band.

Impact had jammed the door, so there was a slight delay embarking as we coaxed it open with a fire axe. A quick walk around old "Annie" was quite revealing. A four foot section of spruce tree was solidly wedged in the nose; an inch was missing from the port propeller tip; and a tree branch had cut into the port wing root, exposing fuel lines. But the most amazing discovery was that the tubular support for both elevators had been cut cleanly under the rudder, while both elevator and stabilizer were missing from the port side. Our trip home had been on one elevator – and a damaged one at that!

Almost immediately a Board of Inquiry was convened, and for several days it looked like we were all destined for the rock pile. Then the tide turned. Arthur's recklessness was seen to be outweighed by his courage and great airmanship. Especially when a team of experts from Avro Aircraft in Toronto completed a minute inspection and submitted their findings. The aircraft was declared unairworthy from the moment it struck the trees. The Board decided that it was only miraculous handling by the pilot which had prevented total disaster.

Arthur's heroics were not exactly sufficient to have him elevated to sainthood – but within a month he was promoted to Flight Sergeant. In many eyes, this promotion was a minor miracle. But the real miracle, I thought, took place quite early that fateful morning – when we climbed aboard a Mark I aircraft.

* * *

The technician on our VHF (very high frequency) test bench in the radio workshop had completed repairs to a radio set and was preparing to check it out. However, when he switched the Baker channel, the main Tower frequency, he found it jammed – apparently by an airborne Harvard whose pilot had inadvertently tripped the transmit switch on his throttle.

There were some muttered imprecations which made it obvious that the pilot was a student, flying on his own. Then there was a stream of very eloquent profanity, ending with the statement: "I'm all buggered up." A moment later the student apparently realized that his transmitter was on, and the carrier went off the air.

Immediately afterwards, the Tower came on. "Aircraft using profanity identify yourself."

After a pause the answer came back, loud and clear: "I'm not that buggered up!"

* * *

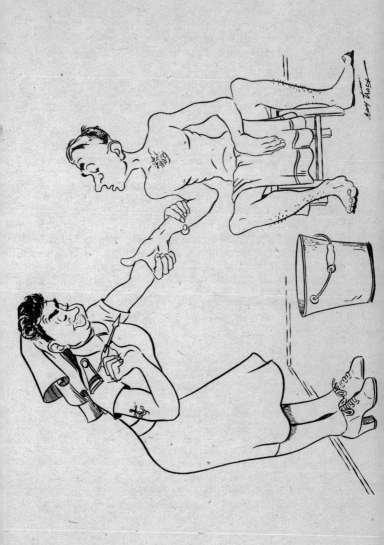

I was posted to Bobbington, an RAF base in England, for navigation training in July 1942. Our course lived in one large tent. It was the worst air force station I was ever on. On arrival, we Canadians were given an introductory speech by an RAF Squadron Leader, who said:

"Let's get something straight. You are now in a civilized country. This is not the wild, wild west. You will be expected to act in conformity with higher standards of behaviour than you would back home."

I've never forgotten that arrival speech because an American kid, the only one in our group, raised his hand and asked if he could make a remark. When it was confirmed that he could speak, he said:

"Sir, I'm an American. And if you dared to include me in those remarks, I'll come up there and whip your ass."

That ended the lecture – and the American made a visit to the Military Prison at Brighton.

I got put on charge twice in the month I was at Bobbington. The first time it was because of the civvy pilots who did the flying for our navigation trainers, and who were always suggesting that we Sergeant navigators were so dumb we wouldn't be able to navigate around the Birmingham barrage balloons. I finally told one of them – in the air – that it would be no loss to Britain if he *did* get entangled in the balloons, since he couldn't steer the course I had given him a minute earlier.

The second charge was over my accusation that the station was stealing the Canadians' chocolate rations. When I threatened to advise Canadian Headquarters in London I was posted straight to an operational squadron – bypassing any Operational Training Unit!

It all ended with me joining No. 35 Pathfinder Squadron, and having the finest time of my life.

* * *

In early summer 1944 it was announced that the RCAF would form sixty four-man crews for the India-Burma theatre. They would operate as separate Canadian transport squadrons learning the supply problems in the Far East prior to a stepped-up war against Japan.

All aircrew in Canada were invited to volunteer – a godsend for the aircrew who had been instructing in Canada ever since they had won their Wings. Champing to get overseas they volunteered in droves.

Among the eager ones was Arthur "Pappy" Deeks. He had been a pilot flying C-47 Dakotas on 164 Communications Squadron at Moncton, New Brunswick, for so long that everyone thought he had invented the Dakota. Somewhat older than most aircrew Pappy was laconic, quiet, competent, and the "best damn knock-rummy player in the RCAF."

Dutifully, he reported to Penfield Ridge, NB, and went through the right-arm-left-arm, left-cheek-right-cheek rumba for tropical innoculation shots; and then he was off to England on the *Empress of Scotland*. Upon arrival at Bournemouth he was almost immediately shipped off to RAF Leicester for a "conversion course" on, of all things, the mighty Dakota aircraft!

Uncomplaining, Pappy went through the ground school classes, and was finally allotted an RAF flying instructor who had just been promoted to Flight Sergeant. The instructor took off, climbed to 4,000 feet, levelled off, and brought the airspeed to 150 knots. He turned to Flight Lieutenant Deeks and asked if he would like to take over the controls. Pappy replied, "Okay."

"Turn to port, maintaining airspeed and altitude," was the instructor's first command. "Turn to starboard, maintaining airspeed and altitude," was the instructor's second command. Then followed a series of turns, climbs, and letdowns – after which the instructor asked Pappy if he would care to bring the aircraft into the circuit. Pappy replied, "Okay."

"Think you can land it?" the instructor asked on the downwind leg.

"I think so," replied Pappy.

Pappy greased it on and then taxied smartly to dispersal, parking exactly where they had originated. The result: a puzzled look from instructor to pupil.

"Just how many hours do you have on DC-3's?"

"About 1,200, I think."

"Jeeesus H. Chroist!" the instructor exploded. "I only have sixty-two hours meself!"

Shortest on the Left

I was the Wing Commander chosen to lead the largest Air Force Parade Winnipeg had ever seen. All of the Training Command was involved. Every officer, every airman, every airwoman, every aircraft, was at my disposal.

Months were spent in preparation for the great day. Rehearsals followed rehearsals, flypasts got bigger and more complicated every day. New and intricate parade patterns were worked out with several thousand troops marching on the cleared concrete aprons in front of the hangars. It was to be a super-colossal production that had top priority and brooked no excuses from anyone. Training Command and the RCAF were going to show the world, especially our NATO partners, that we could put on a show second to none.

Several dress rehearsals were held with the massed bands thumping away and the troops weaving their multiple patterns. Off to the east hundreds of aircraft circled in various orbits, awaiting the signal that would bring them on stage. Each flight of aircraft was preset to perform a particular manoeuvre in harmony with the other flights.

The key to the whole thing lay in my executive order: PARADE. Once I bawled out that order there was no turning back. Everything was timed from that one word. Signals would be flashed to the aircraft and the intricate parade ceremony would be underway with no possibility of reversing the proceedings.

The great day arrived. With the massed troops all drawn up according to plan and the aircraft orbiting their landmarks, with the reviewing stand filled with dignitaries from all NATO countries and the flight line jammed with thousands of spectators, with flags and bunting flapping in the summer breeze – it was an impressive sight.

I stood at attention at the head of the parade with my sword in hand, awaiting the preselected signal that would send me into action. The signal I awaited was rather a simple one. It was the arrival of the Lieutenant-Governor's limousine. He would arrive in a long black limousine and be driven right to the reviewing stand. When I saw the car arrive I was to begin the show.

I waited, feeling the eyes of the world on me. Everything was quiet, everyone was expectant – when out of the corner of my eye I spotted the long black limousine driving sedately in from my right.

In my best parade voice, I roared, "PARADE!" Everything

started – airmen, airwomen, and aircraft – as out stepped the butcher from St. James, an invited guest.

*   *   *

While serving in the RCAF I gathered an earned reputation for avoiding parades. I was called a parade dodger. In retaliation, some sadistic personnel officer transferred me to a very large training station where weekly parades, of a monstrous size, were held in rain or shine.

These were all-out major efforts and all personnel, male and female, trainees and staff, were required to attend. Sometimes there were 3,000 on parade. Following each parade the reviewing officer made special announcements. It was my job to see that he was properly briefed on the contents of these announcements.

On one occasion I asked him to announce that personnel were to cease using the drill hangar walls as a backstop while practising tennis. Too many windows were being broken. I also asked him to remind all training personnel that the sports competition between the courses would resume that evening.

The duty of parade reviewing officer was shared between various senior officers, and the one on this occasion was a bit absent-minded. My worst fears were realized with his first order. "You people are to stop banging your balls against the drill hall walls."

This order resulted in some polite tittering; but his next announcement really broke up the parade in a paroxysm of laughter. "Oh, yes, I am to remind you that the intercourse competition resumes tonight."

*   *   *

Parades had become a way of life at Manning Depot and Trade School, so I found it very strange to arrive at No. 1 Group Headquarters and find no parade or drill activity.

The girls were living in barracks on Torbay Station and the airmen were boarding with civilian families in St. John's. Since we had no parade ground facilities, life was fairly informal in those early days. However, not long after I arrived our adjutant, Flight Lieutenant Joe Canfield, made arrangements with the New-

foundland Hotel authorities to use their tennis courts for drill. These courts were located directly across from the Headquarters building and had not been used since the outbreak of war.

Thereafter, upon arriving at work each morning (coated with a layer of dust from our ride into town on the back of a truck) we were formed into flights on this makeshift drill square and put through our paces.

Flight Lieutenant Canfield had been a Parade Sergeant in the army in 1917 and had lost none of his enthusiasm for bawling out orders. But often he turned these drill sessions over to our young Women's Division officers who had never handled many parades.

One morning our petite Section Officer, Barbara Campbell, was called upon to perform the honours. We were marching at Attention, rapidly approaching the wire fence to the rear of the parade square, and Barbara had obviously forgotten the order for About Turn.

Joe hollered at her: "What do you want them to do, Miss Campbell, climb the fence?"

Barbara, in desperation, croaked, "Hodran Squalt!" We came to a standstill with our noses poking through the wire as our adjutant doubled over in mirth.

After we moved into our new barracks Joe decided to cut back on the daily exercise on the tennis court and we began marching to work each morning with the airmen. The taller men always served as markers, and they would stride out leaving the shorter airwomen to march at double-quick time trying to keep the pace. The girls continued to complain to Joe about this state of affairs and finally, one morning, he found a solution.

He picked three of the shorter airwomen to act as markers. I was one of this trio. Out we strode, completely oblivious to what was going on behind us. When we arrived at Headquarters the boys were panting and puffing and Joe was having himself another great guffaw. This time at the expense of the airmen. Apparently, we had forced them to run all the way. This marked the last of our route marches with the men. The airwomen were formed into flights and would embark on their own route marches.

Some of them were beautiful. At times we would hike up to Signal Hill where we would break ranks for a few minutes to enjoy the terrific view from below Cabot Tower. At other times we might march up King's Bridge Road or down to the harbour. We particularly enjoyed our marches to the harbour because on these occasions we were often invited aboard Allied ships at anchor.

I recall the morning we went aboard a British destroyer to be toured around by a very self-conscious young "subbey" . . . . Two ratings were sitting on a piece of scaffolding above the officer's head, a can of white paint between them as they did touch-up painting. The young officer raised his arm to point out the guns and down came the paint, completely covering his blues. It was a dreadful moment. We wanted to shriek with laughter – but instead we had to contain ourselves and remain perfectly still. The young officer disappeared in the twinkling of an eye and was immediately replaced by an older officer who materialized out of the woodwork without comment, as though rehearsed.

Later, on the bridge, we encountered the younger man again. His hair was streaked with white paint that a rating was attempting to remove with turpentine. It was another proud moment as we exercised perfect control over our mirth.

* * *

My service career in the RAF began in 1939. I was a Boy Entrant at Cranwell. For more than a year our group of boys aged sixteen to seventeen were subjected to a brand of military punishment, called discipline, found only in places like Sandhurst or H.M. Prisons.

When graduation time arrived I was convinced my future held nothing but four hours of square bashing, countless visits to a barber's chair, several kit inspections, and jankers – every day. It was with total surprise, then, that when I was posted to air gunnery training and then an operational squadron, I found a complete absence of parades or irate superiors. Still, I couldn't dispel my doubts that it would end suddenly and I'd be thrust back into the world of high decibel vocal communications, square bashing, and punishments.

In September 1940 I was posted – along with my fears – to No. 2 General Reconnaissance School at Squires Gate, near Blackpool. Here I was immediately detailed for Commanding Officer's parade. Being of small stature I hoped to find a spot in the rear ranks, but in the preliminary shuffling and sizing I was suddenly front and centre.

The state of my health just then was not at its best. I suffered from an acute case of acne pimples and other facial eruptions. Royal Air Force medical science at that time had scarcely progressed beyond Aspirin, the No. 9 pill, and the good doctor's message of hope: "My man, you'll grow out of this."

With thoughts of my initial training fresh in mind, I stood rigidly at attention as our CO, Wing Commander E.A. Blake, made his rounds. He was attended by numerous officers and superfluous help, including "Hoot" Gibson the Sergeant Major, notebook and pencil in hand.

The CO made steady progress down our file until he reached my location – then everything stopped and went quiet. Staring directly in front, I discovered a sea of faces looking at me and my stomach gave a heave. Obviously, my appearance had failed to meet with approval.

"Ah, skin problems, my man?"

"Yes, sir," I replied to the CO.

"Have you been doing anything to treat this?"

"Yes, sir. I went to the Medical Officer and got shots."

"I see! Not doing much good!"

With that, the inspection moved on down the file and I breathed a heavy sigh of relief. But suddenly there was a quick scuffle of gravel as the CO turned around, almost trampling the Sergeant Major, and retraced his steps to my position.

"How old are you, son?" he asked.

"Almost eighteen, sir."

"Do you drink beer?"

Since my upbringing had been strictly temperance, I had been taught that all alcoholic beverages were to be avoided. I was shocked by the question and could only stammer, "No, sir."

"Well, my boy, I'm not suggesting you become a confirmed alcoholic. But I *would* suggest that, since you are underage, someone sneak you the occasional glass of beer. It might help your condition." His parting words, as he ran off to resume his inspection, were: "Malt, malt, malt, you know!"

I soon discovered that the CO's advice was sound. After a few sample glasses my problems were soon over – even though I never acquired a taste for the stuff.

Wing Commander Blake (later Group Captain) was a wonderful humanitarian. And I don't suppose there are very many people who can say that they were introduced to beer on a CO's parade.

*   *   *

While at No. 3 Repair Depot in Vancouver my birthday came around, so I organized myself a large party in town. It was a dandy, and I rolled into barracks just in time for morning parade. Trouble was – I was detailed to call the roll. Things went better than I expected, though, until I came to the name Rourke. No one answered when I bawled out this name. After a pause I yelled it again. No answer.

Then I looked up to see the airmen all smiling and I realized that the name I was calling was my own.

*   *   *

A few months after assuming my command I was "rapped on the knuckles" by Headquarters for not holding weekly Commanding Officer's parades. I was asked to explain why I had not done so, in direct contravention of their written directions on the subject.

With tongue in cheek I replied that it was all a matter of ecology and climate. The black flies and the mosquitoes were too thick and vigorous in the warm weather – and the rest of the year it was too damn cold!

Headquarters' reply to this was that I had their complete sympathy but parade directives were intended to be carried out. I had better get on with weekly parades.

It seemed I had a bit of a problem until I became aware of how they knew I hadn't been holding weekly parades. I learned from my Warrant Officer that a weekly Parade State was to be sent to Headquarters along with each issue of Daily Routine Orders. Headquarters had never received any Parade States.

After I had directed the Warrant Officer to draw up a fictitious Parade State and forward it promptly each week, things got back to normal.

*   *   *

Just as the band swung on to the parade ground a black-and-tan bloodhound emerged from the main entrance of the Trenton Headquarters and took up his position beneath the Standard.

From which vantage point he quietly observed the preliminary proceedings.

Not until the whole parade was in order did he make his next move. He marched across to pay his respects, first to the trumpet band, then to No. 1 Squadron. To the latter he gave the full treatment, inspecting each of the three flights with a thoroughness that must have warmed the heart of the Senior Warrant Officer.

From No. 1 Squadron he moved to No. 2 but, as though sensing the urgency of the moment, he selected only one flight for his scrutiny. Passing rapidly on to No. 3 Squadron he examined number three flight in detail, carrying on in the most correct manner imaginable until, having inspected the full frontage of number two and number one flights, he walked with great dignity and satisfaction back to his former position beneath the flagpole.

On arrival there he was scooped up unceremoniously by a waiting Leading Aircraftman – who was doubtless acting under the orders of someone not fully versed in the protocol of such matters.

For a while it seemed that an inspection begun with such dignity and restraint had come to an ignominious end. But no. The RCAF was dealing with one not lightly overruled. A little later – as the parade marched past in full military order – there, standing proudly on the saluting base, was a black-and-tan bloodhound, a steady light of triumph glowing in his eyes.

* * *

I have frequently been asked if I am Jewish since my surname is one common to both Jews and Gentiles. While in the RCAF I found it advantageous, at times, to pass myself off as Jewish.

During the war, I was attached to an RAF squadron which held periodic Commanding Officer's parades when operational flying permitted. Without the least desire to attend parades, I soon found that indicating I was Jewish would, at least, eliminate church parades. It seemed that the RAF recognized only the Protestant faith. Shortly after a church parade was formed up, the Padre was asked to say a few prayers and the command was given: "Catholics and Jews fall out to the rear!" This gave me the opportunity (heaven sent, I often thought) of bogging-off from the parade.

My greatest "coup" came when I read a notice in Daily Orders

that members of the Jewish faith were entitled to a forty-eight hour pass to observe a forthcoming Jewish holiday. I knew my records were kept at RCAF Headquarters in London so that the squadron would have no way of checking. I foresaw no problem in getting the pass from our Welsh adjutant.

However, old Taffy was a bit more sceptical than I had anticipated, and I had a real moment of apprehension when he asked to see my identification tags. I handed them over while my brain whirled. Taffy looked at them and asked, "What does UCC stand for?"

I told him that the RCAF had anticipated Jewish aircrew would be given a rough time by the Germans if shot down and captured. For that reason, they had the identification tags of all Jewish aircrew stamped with the letters UCC. It meant "Unorthodox Christian of Canada."

I thoroughly enjoyed the forty-eight hour pass that I spent in the fleshpots of London – but my pleasure quickly dissolved when I arrived back at the squadron. One of my RCAF friends, not knowing what I had been up to, had been questioned by the adjutant about the use of UCC on our RCAF dog tags. My friend had told him it meant a member of the United Church of Canada.

Luckily, my friend found me before Taffy did, and warned me to keep out of the way. Taffy was mad. He had made the statement: "When I get my hands on him, I don't care what religion he is. I'll crucify him, anyway!"

* * *

One thing that really bugged me while in the RCAF was parades. To me, parades were a waste of time and effort, taking the troops away from their work. During wartime it was quite noticeable that the reduction in parades was in direct ratio to the closeness of combat.

My feelings about parades were a throwback to the years I had served in the army prior to joining the RCAF. I had purposely avoided the infantry because it seemed to spend most of its time marching around, usually in circles – and had joined the artillery, instead. With their big guns I had not foreseen any need for marching. How wrong I was! An hour on parade in the morning and another in the afternoon. Hell – you couldn't go for a crap unless you marched there!

When I was appointed a Commanding Officer of an RCAF station I thought I had it made: I would simply dispense with parades. It turned out to be no easy task.

Prior to taking over, the CO I was replacing asked what kind of parade I wanted. I suggested that we forget the formalities, but he promptly pointed out that Command Headquarters policy stated that there would be a parade. After much discussion it was agreed that the parade would consist of the two of us at the bar of the Officers' Mess. His only comment was: "It's your funeral. They can't do anything to me. I'm retiring."

A short time later I was asked by Headquarters how my handover parade had gone. I was able to reply with some honesty that it was the most impressive parade I ever attended.

Wizard Trip!

When we were being crewed up at Operational Training Unit our two gunners were the last to join the crew. They were both RAF Sergeants. When they reported to the station they were told to check in the Sergeants' Mess with any pilot who might be looking for crew members.

Our two wizards – Bill from Lancashire and Stan from Yorkshire – approached an Australian Warrant Officer pilot, who had just completed his operational tour and had been screened for instructional duties.

When our heroes asked if he needed any gunners, the Aussie said: "No. I'm a screen." To which the gunners replied: "Yeah, we're a couple of bloody screams, too – but do you need any gunners?"

*   *   *

I was mid-upper gunner on our Halifax bomber, and my time was spent straining into the darkness trying to see German fighters before they saw us. Searching the black sky was a wearying job. Some of our bombing raids lasted seven or eight hours – and that was a long time to concentrate. Especially if your imagination was seeing things your eyes couldn't pick out.

One night, on a raid to the Ruhr Valley, a strange sensation overcame me. A feeling that we weren't alone, that another aircraft was flying alongside the Halifax. Straining into the blackness I concentrated with all my might . . . and gradually I made out the silhouette of a FW 190. The German fighter was almost touching us!

I lined up my guns on it and acquainted the skipper with the situation. "He's less than fifty feet away. Will I let him have it?"

"Geez, no," the skipper answered. "Cripes, you're liable to miss! Don't even breathe, just watch him."

After three or four minutes we were certain that Jerry wasn't aware of our presence. Then a series of flashes and tracers began lacing the sky off to our starboard and the FW 190 peeled off and away towards the action.

When we got back to base we all had a shaky laugh. Sometimes it paid to be too close to the enemy.

*   *   *

On 28 February 1943 our squadron of Wellington bombers was detailed to bomb the submarine pens at St. Nazaire, France, as part of a force of 450 aircraft. We were leaving from Dishforth which was, at that time, a grass field without runways.

Our crew (in which I was the wireless operator) was given "F" for Freddie – a type capable of carrying a "cookie," or 4,000-pound bomb. The weather was ideal with clear skies and light winds. Takeoff was set for 1800 hours, and would be in a westerly direction.

Sergeant Norm Brousseau of Cap de la Madeleine was our skipper, and when he opened the throttles I was standing behind him in the cockpit. We had started to pick up speed halfway in our take-off run when I saw him glancing with concern at the starboard engine. Our speed would not increase. We kept on going just the same – and at the end of the field we found ourselves staring at the Great North Road with only ninety knots on the airspeed indicator!

Norm had no choice but to haul back the stick and try to climb. As the wheels came up I saw ninety-five knots on the clock and thought we had it made. Then Norm said, "I can't hold it up. We're going to hit the ground."

All I could think of was the 4,000-pound bomb in our belly. I closed my eyes, expecting to be blown to Kingdom Come. Instead, we landed softly and smoothly in a farmer's ploughed field. Had I been sitting in my seat, however, I would have been seriously injured. The heavy radio transmitter smashed into the seat on impact. So much for seat belts . . . .

When I walked into the Wireless Section the next morning an RAF bloke said to me: "After this, my friend, I suspect you will survive your tour of ops."

He was right. I survived two tours. Amen.

* * *

I well remember my first operational trip with 425 Squadron at Dishforth in late 1942.

It was a mine-laying operation and we flew into Middleton St. George because the mines couldn't be loaded at Dishforth. Then we were held up by foul weather and didn't take off for three days.

Each day we were briefed and ready for takeoff – and each day the trip was scrubbed at the last minute. Each day we were given two large chocolate bars as our quick energy ration . . . . On the night we finally took off I had six chocolate bars stuffed into my flying suit.

I was so high-strung and nervous by the time we got away that I can hardly remember dropping the mines. We flew through a lot of naval flak but got away safely – and in my relief I ate the six bars on the flight home. To my everlasting embarrassment my first operational trip ended with me bent over in the dispersal, honking up six chocolate bars.

*   *   *

While flying with an RAF Beaufort Torpedo Bombing Squadron at the end of 1940, one of our tasks was known as Gardening. It consisted of sowing 1,000-pound light case mines in waters frequented by enemy shipping, and was done at night. It was a highly dangerous job since you were flying so close to the enemy's shore.

In order that the fragile missile would not be damaged and rendered useless, it was dropped at low level and at the slowest speed possible. Navigation had to be precise and the pilots had to fly accurately on instruments. The aircrews didn't much care for the job since casualties were high.

On one night the takeoff was set for 2100 hours with briefing at 1930 hours. A rather morose lot of us gathered in the briefing hut at the appointed time. The briefing officer was a portly, pipe-smoking, good-natured RAF Squadron Leader wearing an observer's Wing and ribbons won in World War One. At the end of his operational spiel, he thought he would enliven the proceedings.

"All right, chaps," he said. "Watch out for flak, night fighters, high sand dunes, and low tides. Be sure you're between the Frisian Islands and the mainland. Off you go. Good luck and good hunting. If I were twenty years younger I'd be with you myself but now I'll be off to the Mess for a stiff whiskey and two hours of hysterical laughter."

Nobody even smiled.

*   *   *

All fighter pilots prided themselves on wearing a crushed and battered hat. The more it sagged over the ears the more operational it looked. It was the same with the top button on their tunics. No self-respecting Spit pilot would be seen dead with his top button fastened. Irreverence was the hallmark of the professional fighter pilot – and it manifested itself in the most benign settings.

RAF Kenley was a prewar station, but early in the war it became a vital part of Britain's air defences. The Officers' Mess was a long, low, ivy-clad building. The lounge was furnished with deep, black-leather sofas and easy chairs, heavy wooden tables, and rich drapes. The dining room, with its dark refectory tables and heavy carved wooden chairs and side tables, was full of lovely silver. In the lounge, magazines such as *London Opinion, Lilliput, London Illustrated* and, of course, copies of *Punch* were scattered about. The impression given was that of an exclusive club (as indeed it was) and except for the distant snarl of Merlin engines as Spitfires reached for the sky, the atmosphere was scholastic. The age of the young pilots only added to that atmosphere.

It was in a far corner of this Mess on a day shortly after the Battle of Britain that a high-ranking Canadian officer, fresh from Canada, was being received by a group of young RCAF pilots. It was evident from his ribbons and well-worn pilot's Wings that the officer had seen action in World War One.

He was taking the opportunity of his captured audience to instruct the young pilots on their sundry shortcomings. He objected strenuously, for example, to the removal of the wire stiffener from their hats. "Makes you all look like cab drivers!" he huffed. The pilots were all listening politely and taking his admonitions good-humouredly – until he stated that flying a Spitfire was essentially a sedentary occupation. He recommended daily exercise and allowed that swimming was perhaps the best exercise for a fighter pilot.

Standing in the group was one of the RCAF's top fighter pilots with the unlikely name of "Bitsy" Grant. He had been an intercollegiate wrestling champion at Queen's University and had kept himself in excellent physical condition. Grant took an impish delight in baiting people, particularly senior types, and he had developed a long and skilful needle. He leaned forward and said eagerly, "Sir, I was swimming the other day."

"Good show!" snorted the senior officer. "Went to the Baths at Perley, did you?"

"No, sir," replied Grant disingenuously. "I was in the Channel for two hours."

Our squadron flew Halifax III's powered by the Hercules radial engines. They were good aircraft, and our crew much preferred them to the old Merlin-engined Hally's. I was the tail gunner.

One night on a saturation raid over Germany we got really clobbered by flak, and our skipper gave the order to bail out. I followed all the laid-down procedures of unstrapping, rotating my turret, unplugging the oxygen and intercom, and snapping on my chest parachute pack. Then I let myself fall out backwards from the turret.

As soon as I felt that I was free of the aircraft I pulled the ripcord – but I had released too soon. My feet were still wedged in the turret. Struggling to gather the parachute and fight my way back I was pummelled and whipped by the slipstream as the wildly gyrating Halifax fell out of control through the black sky.

Finally, with a desperate and panic-stricken heave, I worked my way back to a position where I could unfasten my flying boots – and then I fell out of *them*. But the worst was yet to come. I began falling through wave after wave of oncoming bombers. I was parachuting through the bomber stream!

With each passing bomber my parachute would be stretched out horizontally, and I would be sucked along in the vortex caused by the aircraft. Then, as I straightened out and began to fall vertically again, another bomber would drag me after it. I was whipped all over the night sky. The noise was fantastic and I was certain that the next bomber would slice me in two with its propellers.

After what seemed like a lifetime I finally hit the ground. When my head cleared I found that I had landed near a high wall. It turned out to be a German army barracks. Dumping my chute, I groped along the wall until I came to a driveway with a gate . . . . When I went through it I walked smack into two German sentries!

They challenged me – but I grunted a guttural reply and kept walking. I was maybe fifty feet away from them before they both roared for me to halt.

They had finally noticed that I wasn't wearing any boots.

*   *   *

A World War One ditty that we sang in France went to the tune of

"The Dark Town Strutters Ball." (The Hungry Lizzie was the ambulance.)

> *I'll be around to get you in the Hungry Lizzie*
> *Pick up all I find;*
> *I may leave some behind –*
> *But you can fix that up with the undertaker.*
> *We'll do the slow march for you,*
> *And dig a little hole right in the ground;*
> *And on your tombstone we'll have cut*
> *He was a damn fine pilot but*
> *He went to pieces when he spun into the ground.*

* * *

One night, when we were returning from a raid on Berlin, our Lancaster was diverted to Burn because of bad weather at Linton. Burn was a bomber base located south of York.

The next day the station was so busy getting ready for that night's operation that there was no time to gas up our aircraft. Our crew sat out on a wing of "O" Oboe, away from the wind, enjoying some February sun.

As we waited, the talk got around to 408 Squadron losses and our chances of finishing our tour of ops. Someone said, "The law of averages is against us . . . ."

To keep up morale (although I firmly believed he was right) I said, "What do you mean, law of averages?" And I made the point – which I wasn't at all sure was correct – that if you toss a coin and it turns up heads fifty times in a row, the chances of it turning up heads on the fifty-first toss are exactly the same as the first toss. "It's all a question of skill," I added. "We've got one of the best pilots on the squadron, and certainly the best navigator! Now if you gunners will just keep your eyes open we'll make it."

My remarks were greeted with much derision but I think they did help a little.

One of the crew then began to talk about how, on 408 Squadron, few of the crews who had converted to Lancs from Halifaxes were still around. The last to go missing was Flight Lieutenant Reg Laine and his crew.

"Oh, but their navigator kept a list," a gunner piped up. "And that's bad luck."

I didn't mention that I was also keeping a list. I have it in front of me, now. In fact, I kept three lists . . . .

The first list shows target, track miles, bomb loads, the number of aircraft committed to the raid, and the number missing – according to the British Broadcasting Corporation. The BBC didn't include bombers that had ditched in the North Sea or that had crashed in England. In their terminology, the bombers weren't missing. The crews might be dead – but the bombers themselves were not missing. (For example, on 16 December 1943 we made a Berlin raid and, on our return, found most of northern England solidly fogged in. The BBC announced that thirty aircraft were missing from the night's raid – but thirty-six bombers had also crashed in England. Two of the crashes had been at our base at Linton.)

The second list shows the names of pilots and navigators of missing aircraft. And the third list covers the names of those who made it through a tour of ops. I notice that I am number twenty-two out of a total of 220. That's one in ten odds.

My brother did his tour in No. 3 Group and, during his tour, his squadron lost sixty-six crews – a total of 462 airmen. These were worse odds than mine.

*   *   *

Since so many of our bombers came limping home from raids over Germany, all shot up and ready to crash-land all across England, several very large landing strips were built to handle the cripples.

It was a good idea. A number of these giant runways were built near the coast of the North Sea. They could handle a bomber that had had its brakes shot away, and were equipped to remove the plane from the airstrip if it had to crash-land. The runways were lined with pipes that could burn 100-octane gasoline. The heat from the flames could clear fog to a height of 100 feet, and this system (called FIDO) saved countless bombers and their crews.

Each of the fields had USAF, RAF, and RCAF detachments to service their own aircraft. I was stationed for a time at Woodbridge in Suffolk – the first field to be built – where we had about thirty Canadians to care for any of our kites that landed in. We had two Airspeed Oxfords and one Avro Anson aircraft, two pilots, a technical officer, and assorted tradesmen (airframe and

aero-engine mechanics, instrument techs, electricians, and the like). We lived in three Nissen huts strung together on one site. An island of Canadians in a sea of Limeys and Yanks.

As well as the kites that landed at Woodbridge we serviced any aircraft that had had to land somewhere away from its own base. Jumping into the Anson or Oxford, we flew to the rescue, serviced it, and saw it safely off for base. I thought it a great job. Plenty to do. Plenty of time off. Lots of diversions. And no BS, parades, or drill.

One day early in 1945 we were told to paint invasion stripes on our aircraft. Then we were instructed to wear "Combined Operations Badges" on our uniforms. This was a cloth badge depicting an anchor and propeller entwined underneath a crown. It was to be sewn on the right sleeve just above the wrist. Very neat.

For me, getting a "dodad" to wear on my uniform in wartime was the equivalent of a new suit to a civvy. I was proud and excited – even though I didn't know what it meant or why there was such a hurry to paint the aircraft.

I never did find out! I was posted the next day to 408 Squadron at Linton-on-Ouse. There a young sprog Flying Officer told me to take it off. He said I wasn't entitled to wear it.

*　　*　　*

One night, in April 1944, we lost an engine on our Stirling bomber and had to divert to Thorney Island on our return. This was a fighter station flying Typhoons and nobody knew how to repair a Hercules engine.

We hitched a ride back to our base the next morning to pick up groundcrew and the necessary tools and bits and pieces. Since the squadron couldn't loan us a spare aircraft we took the train back down to Thorney Island – and this created another diversion.

Our skipper, who lived in London, insisted that we all stay overnight at his home. So we trooped dutifully to his house in the northeast part of town. Once there, the skipper insisted that we all visit his favourite pub. We were all in flying gear and the groundcrew were all in working dress and no one was ready for an evening on the town. But that's what we got.

It was a memorable night. At one point, the mid-upper gunner was standing on the bar trying to auction off his flying boots for beer money. Then, on the way home, we picked up some girls who began to have a great time blowing our dinghy whistles and flashing our three-cell flashlights. Immediately, we were pounced on by some Bobbies and air raid wardens – who were all for locking us up for the night.

It was the skipper's uncle who saved us. We had just been shot down, he proclaimed, and were on our way back to our squadron.

*   *   *

We had a crew on our squadron who landed back at base minus their mid-upper gunner. They had encountered heavy opposition over Germany and, in escaping from the German fighters, had used up most of their fuel. The skipper decided to take a shortcut over London to save some gas.

Unfortunately, they got caught in the middle of a German raid on London and took a severe pounding from their own flak guns. The skipper ordered everyone to prepare to abandon aircraft, but the mid-upper gunner didn't wait for the actual order to jump. He bailed out immediately. Meanwhile, the pilot managed to escape the barrage and fly on to base.

As soon as the gunner got back to base he went LMF (Lack of Moral Fibre) and refused to fly again. When he had landed in London by parachute he had been set upon by irate Londoners who assumed he was German. He had to be rescued by air raid wardens and police. He said that if his own people would do that to him he could imagine what the Germans would do if he ever bailed out over Germany. That ended his flying career.

*   *   *

We were flying Stirling bombers on special operations and had just returned from a trip. Getting out of the aircraft at dispersal, we saw another Stirling taxiing into its dispersal point alongside. Suddenly, as the aircraft cut its motors, the rear gunner flipped out of his turret and landed with a sickening thud on his head, his parachute billowing over him.

Our crew ran over to see what was going on and found the tail gunner out cold. As the pilot climbed down, we found out what had happened.

They had been flying close to the enemy coast in range of the German flak batteries, and the aircraft had suffered a great deal of damage. The rear gunner's oxygen and heat had been cut off in the shooting. Unsure that he could keep the Stirling flying, the skipper had warned the crew to prepare to abandon ship. But after a time he got things organized and was able to fly back to base. Meanwhile, the rear gunner had fallen asleep through cold or lack of oxygen.

The landing must have jarred him awake – and when they rolled into dispersal he was still groggy. As the engines stopped the skipper had yelled out his customary, "Okay, guys. Bail out!" Which the gunner did, receiving a mild concussion and weeks of ribbing.

*   *   *

No. III Squadron – or Treble One as it was called by everyone who served on it – was prestigious even before it was posted, after the Battle of Britain, to North Africa. In its new location it became the spearhead of a Fighter Wing located in the Medjerda Valley, strategically placed to cover the final assault on Tunis: the successful attack which would completely banish the Axis forces from North Africa.

Treble One was also known as the Nelson squadron; one eye, one arm, one asshole. It was located between two market villages, Souk el Arba and Souk el Khemus; ("souk" meaning market in the Arabic language). The runways were made from sections of steel matting laid on the sand, and the days were filled with a clattering of tires on steel mesh in the middle of a bowl of blowing sandy dust.

The pilots were billeted in a Tunisian farmhouse near Souk el Arba. The kitchen became the Mess. Those who didn't rate a kip in the farmhouse were billeted under canvas in a grove of eucalyptus.

While Treble One was officially an RAF squadron it was, in fact, a motley collection of many nationalities. Canadians made up the largest portion of the foreign contingent – which included Rhodesians, South Africans, Australians, New Zealanders, and one Icelandic pilot. However, the core of Treble One remained English.

Whenever the RAF originals felt threatened (as they sometimes did) by the proliferation of Commonwealth comrades, they would

reaffirm their identities by appearing with shoulder-flashes which read "England." It was the English pilots who gave the squadron the characteristics and sounds of an English public school. The squadron cheerfully referred to lesser breeds within their ranks as "colonials" or "black troops" and to themselves as the "Dreaded Treble One." They borrowed their language from public school talk, which was entwined with RAF slang so that a prang became a "prangers-ho" and gin was "ginners-ho." Added to this mélange was a salty dash of rhyming cockney and scraps of Greek, French, and Latin – all designed to isolate Treble One as well as protect it culturally.

One of the traditions of the squadron was the "boozers-ho" which took place when the NAAFI (Navy Army Air Force Institute) came through with the monthly allotment of liquor. One bottle – per officer – per month – perhaps. It was an occasion for a monstrous bash, complete with singsong *and* an iron-clad rule that songs could not be sung after the booze had been scoffed. It only took one night to dispose of the monthly supply.

Once, while killing time, a Canadian pilot found a way to improve the amenities of the farmhouse Mess. A former bush pilot and self-reliant to a fault, he discovered a technique for cutting empty beer bottles down to the size of mugs. The vocabulary of the Mess was enhanced from that moment. No longer did one take a drink; one "lowered a jar."

There was an occasion when Treble One was ordered to mount a two-aircraft reconnaissance patrol with the code name, Yellow Section. The two Spitfires were led by a young RCAF Pilot Officer, and his wingman was a newly-arrived Flight Sergeant – described by an observer as a fear-crazed sprog. Their patrol would be monitored by Badger – a new radar installation buried deep in a hillside bunker. Shortly after they were airborne, Badger called Yellow Leader.

"I say, Yellow Leader, Badger here. We have twenty-plus bandits heading your direction. I say, let's have a party. We can put you right onto them. Over."

On hearing this news, the Pilot Officer sensibly changed direction 180 degrees, which would prevent any confrontation with this German circus.

Undismayed, Badger continued to blow the hunting horn. "I say, Badger here. Have you seen the bandits, Yellow Leader?"

Yellow Leader was, by this time, almost safely back to base. He remained silent.

Badger continued to press for an attack with repeated calls, all of which were ignored. Finally, Badger began pleading, "Yellow Leader, Yellow Leader. Come in, Yellow Leader."

As the runway came into sight, Yellow Leader pressed his microphone button. "This is the yellowest goddamn leader you will never see, Badger," he said.

Treble One was paid a tribute by an English war correspondent, who wrote a laudatory book entitled *They Flew Through Sand*. It was, of course, immediately retitled by the squadron members in their self-depreciatory style. They called it *They Flit Through Shit*.

* * *

Now that many RCAF veterans are reaching retirement age, they are making pilgrimages to their old overseas haunts. For some it is a marvellous experience to revisit the old stations and airfields, the villages and towns and townspeople . . . sharing the visit with husband or wife and children. For others, the visits are too poignant, too disturbing and emotion-wracked, and they turn away forever.

Some freely admit that such travels are an attempt to recapture the youth so recklessly spent in those war years. Some say that they go just to catch a glimpse of a half-remembered vision. For all of them it's a voyage back to yesterday, where often long-forgotten agonies and heartbreaks lie in wait. Hiding there, too, are unexpected delights that can make the spirits soar and roll the years away.

The same pub owner, still holding forth – or the man who ran the fish-and-chip shop, anxious to talk about the days of your youth and to offer insights about incidents you never knew happened. A well-known face, a building, a country road, a familiar sound, or a simple combination of weather and landscape, can bring floods of tears or gales of laughter. A long-abandoned, weed-infested runway. The airmen's huts, their iron rusting, their doors ajar. All of these can start up the echoes of past days, and send vibrations down your spine that shake the years within you.

In another sense, the desire to go back is a matter of curiosity, of wanting to know: *Did it all really happen?* It is an attempt, in many ways, to bring those days down to size, back into your life where they can be understood. Then, too, some travellers have a special purpose in going back. They are taking the opportunity to thank others for an action that was made, long ago, on their behalf . . . . Bill Barry of Edmonton took the long trip back to those days in 1942, when he was a Pilot Officer navigator on RAF 192 Squadron, based at Gransden Lodge. One of the reasons for Bill's trip was his desire to find and thank the fishermen who had saved his crew from drowning in the English Channel.

It was 8:00 A.M. on 3 December 1942, and Frank Arnold and Roland Raines were at sea off Kingsdown, Kent, fishing for sprats. Frank Arnold had been given a special gap in the anti-invasion defences on the beach to get his boat through, and he and his nephew, Roland, were at sea as often as the winter weather permitted.

It was a surprisingly calm morning and they were paying out their nets when, suddenly, the sound of a low-flying aircraft shattered the stillness. It approached them from the north and was down almost to sea level. Thinking it was a German raider, and anticipating a stream of bullets, the two men got ready to crouch in the bottom of their small craft, hoping for what little shelter it would afford. Then the plane hit the water about a half mile away from them.

Without stopping to think of whether the crew were English or German, the two men went to the rescue. Frank Arnold cut away the sprat nets and Roland Raines started the engines. Within a matter of minutes, the tiny Kingsdown boat was alongside the Wellington bomber which had flopped, like a great, wounded bird, into the sea. The bomber was sinking fast – and the Kingsdown boatmen wasted no time in taking the five crew members, who had climbed onto the wing, into their small craft.

Three of the crew (they were all Canadians) were badly wounded, and they were handled gently. The little sprat boat was now well-laden, its gunwales almost awash. Although there was no medical or first aid equipment aboard, the wounded were made as comfortable as possible and a start was made for the shore.

In itself, the rescue was not extraordinary. It was just one of hundreds taking place around the coast of Britain during the war. What makes the rescue historic is that the Wellington was no ordinary bomber.

A special decoy aircraft, it was sent up on the instructions of Professor Lindeman, later Lord Cherwell, in an effort to obtain details of the deadly radar equipment known as Lichtenstein. This equipment was fitted to German night fighters and made them highly efficient. In addition to its regular crew of five, the Wellington also carried a special wireless operator.

Over the Dutch coast, and over Germany, the aircraft had deliberately courted danger that dark night. Time and again it had been attacked by German night fighters, and four of the crew members were wounded as a result of the fighter attacks. But it accomplished its mission – the all-important details of the German radar had been obtained. Although the special wireless operator had been badly wounded, he had made accurate observations; and these proved to be of inestimable value to the scientists working to unravel the Luftwaffe night-defence system.

The work done that night by the Wellington and its crew was important enough for Sir Winston Churchill to record it in his memoirs: *The Second World War* (volume IV, chapter XVI). Churchill described Lichtenstein as the one detail that had still been missing in the mystery of German air defence, and it was, he wrote, "imperative to find out more about it." Churchill gave all praise to the crew:

On the night of December 2, 1942, an aircraft of 192 Squadron was presented as a decoy. It was attacked many times by an enemy night fighter radiating the Lichtenstein transmissions. Nearly all the crew were hit. The special operator listening to the radiations was severely wounded in the head, but continued to observe with accuracy. The wireless operator, though badly injured, was parachuted out of the aircraft over Ramsgate, and survived with the precious observations. The rest of the crew flew the plane out to sea and alighted on the water because the machine was too badly damaged to land on an airfield. They were rescued by a boat from Deal. The gap in our knowledge of the German night defences was closed.

Pilot Officer Barry spent three days in Deal hospital before he could return to base – so he remembered it well when he returned to Deal in 1983 to thank the two brave fishermen who had saved the lives of him and his comrades . . . . But it was not to be. Both had long since died. Barry, however, did get the satisfaction of meeting the son of one of the rescuers – Tony Arnold – who showed him a copy of a long-forgotten letter that he had sent to his rescuers . . . . It has been Tony Arnold's story, written for the East Kent *Mercury* newspaper, that you have just read.

Was his long trip back worth the effort in time and emotion? Bill Barry said: "Just being there again and seeing everything, and especially meeting the son of the man who rescued us from the sea, made it all worthwhile. I'm so glad I went."

War Games

The Wing Commander was gruff in a gentlemanly way, as are most graduates from military academies; but this one's gruffness was awe-inspiring in moments of pique. As a subordinate commander I was not, at any time, in fear of the man. Rather, I admired him shamelessly, as a much-decorated hero of an earlier war.

One morning in 1943 I had no sooner sat down to my daily routine of processing aircrew for further combat training when the telephone rang. It was a summons to the Old Man's carpet. He was furious.

He informed me with stentorian authority that one of my aircrew trainees had better be corrected – and demanded that I should see to it personally and immediately. I was advised that during the night a young Sergeant air gunner had trampled through the fountain, damaging the goldfish, the water lilies, and the King's uniform.

I sensed that a group of frustrated aircrew, awaiting posting to Operational Training Units, had vented some steam in the local English pubs. Returning to the serenity of my office, I ordered the main miscreant paraded.

What a shock was to greet me.

If this child was more than fifteen years old I would be greatly surprised. Noticing his extreme nervousness I told the police escort to withdraw, and proceeded to question the young Sergeant alone. He told me he had "got kinda high" with his buddies. Yes, sir, he had smashed through the fountain. No, he was seventeen-and-a-half, sir.

As I sat listening to him, disbelieving he was even that old, I decided that the best procedure would be to move him on to advanced training immediately. When I asked him if he would like an immediate posting he replied, "As soon as possible, sir!"

The next draft roll was on my desk, and the train would be leaving in one hour. I ordered him to go to stores and be kitted to scale and then to report to the Warrant Officer in charge at the railway station. Later that day the Warrant Officer advised me that "young Jones" had left on schedule.

The Wing Commander was happy to be rid of a punishment case. I was happy to accord him this pleasure. The young lad was happy to be on his way to war.

All this happened on a Sunday.

On Monday morning there was a Confidential and Personal letter in my mail. It was from a very senior personnel officer at RCAF Overseas Headquarters, directing action as appropriate on a copy of a handwritten letter from Canada . . . .

"Would you please send back my boy," the letter read. "He wanted so badly to join the air force that his father and I falsified his age for him. But since he is not yet fifteen could you *please* not let him go to war?" The letter was signed "Mrs. Jones" – and it left no doubt that she was referring to the boy who had damaged the goldfish pond and was now very close to going to war indeed.

A quick conference with the Wing Commander was imperative. Protocol was the punctilious order of the day. There could be no lateral correspondence with another command and, anyway, the lad's next course of training was of four weeks' duration. So: best preserve military correctness and advise Headquarters in London that "Sergeant Jones" was, as of yesterday, transferred to operational training at "Biddington-Mountford." Whether this decision was made from sympathy for the rules was mutually unstated. But that was the procedure adopted.

All this happened on a Monday.

A week passed – and then it was Tuesday, the tenth day, and still no "Sergeant Jones" had appeared for processing to Canada, home, and parents. A discussion about when we should see him on parade in my office had been a breakfast opener every morning.

The tenth day was the day.

Shortly before noon the Warrant Officer, wreathed in smiles, announced that "Sergeant Jones" requested to be paraded. Restraining any tendency to look eager I granted the request, and before me came "Sergeant Jones" – saluting and wearing a brand new ribbon of the Distinguished Flying Medal!

"It happened like this, sir," he explained. "I knew Mum would have written soon because she said she would in her last letter. Well, I wasn't keen to let the fellows know how young I was, and I sure didn't want to go home, so I cooked it. For the first time, I got high. I walked through the Wing Commander's pool on a bet. My own bet – not theirs!

"I knew the Wing Commander would be mad, but I guessed you would be the one to punish me. I figured if I got before you on a charge you might draft me out. I was right. When I got to operational training I had the chance to join a crew graduating to a squadron. On the first night we went on a bombing mission, and I shot down a Jerry. On Saturday I was awarded the DFM. So now, sir, what do you want to do with me?"

To say I was flabbergasted would be a small understatement. Here, standing before me, was a fifteen year old – a winner of an immediate award of the Distinguished Flying Medal. What comedy of errors could have constructed this situation? The thought of him going home without the Ceremony of Investiture at the Palace was too much. After all, he had won his DFM through great skill and courage.

A pact must be made.

A letter was composed in which it was explained how this youthful, courageous, and thoroughly devoted warrior should have his wish granted: to be officially invested, repatriated to his proud parents by a grateful air force, and released from further duty until coming of age.

I don't know where that young man is now. I can't even remember his correct name. Perhaps he will read this and recognize himself.

* * *

An Intelligence Officer stationed at Blida, a coastal station near Algiers, sought to confuse and baffle the Germans. He gave the station a code name. He called it Hemorrhage.

* * *

I remember when I was working on the Yank base at Fort Pepperell and a group of German soldiers, disguised as Americans, infiltrated the Headquarters.

One of them was caught going through the files. When he was questioned, his ID dog tags failed to jive with anyone stationed there, and he was escorted to the jug. Before he had time to alert any of the others, General Brookes called General Assembly on the parade square. While all the units were assembled and the roll call taken, the Military Police searched the empty buildings and rounded up the rest of the Germans. They had been put ashore by U-boats in a remote part of the peninsula. All could speak fluent

English – and all had spent considerable time in the United States before the war. It brought the war overseas a lot closer to us.

We often listened to Lord Ha Ha's radio broadcasts from Germany, and I remember one time when he directed his entire broadcast to the Allied forces stationed at St. John's. He correctly told us what movies were currently playing in all the theatres in St. John's – as well as in our own theatre, right on the base!

The Germans used to boast that they put submarine crews ashore in Halifax, crews that could walk down the streets and never be detected. This didn't sound unrealistic to me, for there were so many foreign ships in port that foreign uniforms were a common sight. No one paid any attention. No one ever thought that they might be Germans . . . .

*   *   *

We worked closely in Halifax with the American 685th Signal Company – and they loved to give the Canadians a hard time about our lack of security precautions. When they were transferred to St. John's, Newfoundland, they actually had to go to Boston before they could catch ship.

They were boarded on a ship in the middle of a dark night, after being delivered to the docks in a blacked-out train. Everything was hush-hush. Two days out they were rammed in a pea-soup fog by another ship in their convoy and received terrific damage. The convoy sailed off – but they had to limp into Halifax, taking water and listing badly. They were leaving a wide wake behind them, so there were some anxious hours. (This was when the waters off Nova Scotia were teeming with U-boats; and it was about this time, too, that the Newfie ferry, *The Caribou*, was sunk. They were pretty scary days.)

When they finally reached Halifax the Americans were housed at the "Y" depot, where I also happened to be living. They stayed until after Christmas. When they left, a great send-off was organized. They were paraded to the docks with a navy band, and the curbs of the city were lined with cheering Haligonians, anxious to give them a hearty *bon voyage*.

Those guys of the 685th couldn't believe it! They could never account for the so-called lack of security by their Canadian hosts. It was such a contrast to their departure from Boston . . . . Just the same, they got to St. John's without any trouble at all.

*   *   *

Censorship was tight in Newfoundland throughout the war years, for this was considered overseas service. Newfoundland was a part of Britain at the time. I was an airwoman, and I worked in the Filter Operations Centre as a plotter. Our Filter facilities were located on the American base at Fort Pepperell, where we worked together with members of the American Signal Corps attached to the Army Air Corps.

In our letters home, we were not allowed to write anything about our work. The word "radar" was never mentioned. This tight censorship was always puzzling to the girls because when we went on leave we would very often discover articles on the front pages of our hometown papers which dealt with those "top secret" activities we were forbidden to mention in our letters.

Once, an airwoman who worked with me received a book from her Dad. Published by the government, and entitled *Home War*, it discussed the full scope of our work while outlining the activities of the North Atlantic squadrons. It even had a section covering our Operational Filter Room – with photographs of us working the plots!

I suppose it wasn't the overall stuff that was worth censoring, but the hour-by-hour movements of the convoys and aircraft. It must have been felt that if we were not permitted to write *anything* in our letters which had to do with our work, then there would be no risk of us going into details.

But who wanted to write home about work, anyway? Not with all those single men around!

*   *   *

I was shot down on 3 November 1943 while flying a Whitley bomber from No. 24 Operational Training Unit at Honeybourne. It was a leaflet raid over France.

I parachuted successfully to earth and evaded capture by hiding during the day and walking at night. Fortunately, I could speak the French language – and after three weeks of dodging around the country, I made contact with the Resistance movement. They out-fitted me with a false passport and other identification papers, and dressed me in civilian clothes.

82

I was taken by train to Caen, and then Paris; finally ending up at Maquis D'L'Ain, in the Jura mountains near the Swiss border. I was to spend six months with the Maquisard and to become known to them as "Canada." They would kid me about the mission of "dropping toilet paper" which had brought me to France. Looking back, my experiences with them consisted of 40 per cent fear, 20 per cent hunger, 20 per cent loneliness, 19 per cent cold, and 1 per cent comedy. Although the fear percentage rose to 90 per cent on several occasions.

I hadn't been with them long before the Maquis decided that it would be advantageous if they all had a knowledge of English. They thought this would be a help when the Allied invasion took place. I was asked if I would instruct them, and – not having a hell of a lot to do – I decided to take on the challenge. None of the French knew one word of English, so they naturally believed everything I taught them. Including a few phrases I invented for my own amusement.

The first thing they learned from me was the universal greeting they should use each time they met someone: *Fuck you*.

At the dinner table when they wished the bread they were to say: *Kiss my ass*.

If they wished the cheese they were to say: *Ram it up your ass*.

When meeting any of the Allies they were to greet them with a hearty handshake and: *Hello, you son-of-a-bitch*.

Luckily, I was able to keep a straight face; but this ability was tested and taxed on many occasions, especially when I would overhear my comrades practising their pronunciation. Often, I was startled by their morning greeting of "Fuck you!" At other times I would become confused, and when I would be asked to pass the cheese I would pass the bread. Then they would swear at me and berate me with, "No, no, not 'kiss my ass' but 'ram it up your ass.'"

There were a few other inaccuracies I imparted to my eager students. But on the whole I did teach them a lot of correct English . . . .

Fifteen years after I returned to civilian life, a former Maquis pupil, nicknamed Bill, arrived at my home in Ottawa. He had a great steamer trunk filled with pots and pans and knives and axes and tents and other outdoor equipment to help him survive in the wilds of Canada. I suspect that if it had been legally possible he would have brought his Maquis arsenal of Sten gun, grenades, and explosives.

The reason he was so equipped, it seemed, was because of my Maquis days spent around the campfires. I must have mentioned my log cabin in the wilderness – and how we had beat off countless Indian attacks on our settlement in Ottawa.

My Maquis comrade had arrived in Canada by boat and train, and he had diligently practised his English on one and all of his travelling companions. He said that he was very pleased to see me after meeting so many unsociable Canadians. Particularly in the dining car of the train. I, however, had forgotten the English lessons I had taught him – until we sat down to our own dinner with my wife and two small children. Immediately, a crash retraining program was launched! After some long and hard work I felt he was now ready for contact with our friends and neighbours.

I took Bill on a walk to show him our neighbourhood, and we stopped at a friend's house so introductions could be made. My neighbour's wife *and* his mother-in-law were greeted with: "Hello, you son-of-a-bitch!" as he shook hands with them. Obviously, I had forgotten that salutation in the retraining program.

One evening we decided to build a bonfire in the backyard and so relive the old Maquis days. We had a great evening as we raised our glasses recalling the good times as well as the horrible ones. During our reminiscences, Bill said, "Remember how brave you were when the barn caught on fire? Remember? You stayed and put the fire out by yourself."

I recalled the time – and I still wondered why my comrades had fled so quickly from the barn when the fire started. I hadn't been at all concerned. I couldn't see any danger of being trapped if I didn't get the blaze under control. Nor did I know why the Maquis were watching me from such a great distance.

Now I found out. I had, Bill insisted, been most courageous – knowing that all our bombs and ammunition were hidden under the hay. The trouble was, I hadn't known until that moment about our bombs and ammunition under the hay! Had I known I would have fled farther and faster than my comrades.

On another occasion during our talks we recalled the German attacks against our Maquis camps in April 1944. The Germans had kept us continually on the move, and after a week of constantly finding new camp sites we had ended up in a pine forest making shelters in the snow out of pine boughs. We had remained holed up in that position for a week – and as Bill talked, I recalled pulling some practical jokes on the men: tying their shoelaces together when they slept and throwing snowballs at them and generally doing what any Canadian boy of nineteen would do for amusement. Bill insisted that I had kept up the morale of the camp with my hi-jinks in the pines – knowing that the Germans had us completely surrounded in our little forest.

I hadn't realized, of course, until he told me, that we had been in such dire peril. Had I known I would have been the most worried Maquisard. And my fear percentage would have climbed to 99 per cent!

That Men May Fly

It would be marvellous if we could look back and say that air-women were eagerly welcomed into the RCAF in 1939 when World War Two began.

Nothing, unfortunately, could be further from the truth. Although there were many skilled women – including pilots – available and clamouring for the opportunity to join, the hide-bound service persisted in its male-only prerogative.

It took an acute shortage of manpower, plus the urging of the RAF, to nudge the Canadian government towards improving its rules. But it happened only after a year-long study had been made. Then, and only then, was authority granted to form a female component of the RCAF. Finally, on 2 July 1941, the Canadian Women's Auxiliary Air Force was born (CWAAF).

Little has been written about the women who volunteered for service in the RCAF during the war – or those who followed in peacetime, for that matter. Over 17,000 saw service at home or overseas in the war years. Possibly the only tribute to their magnificent service was the one commissioned by the RCAF (Women's Division) Association of Hamilton, when Mary Ziegler wrote a well-received book called *We Serve That Men May Fly*. This was the slogan used by the recruiters throughout World War Two, and the one that became the women's war cry. Perhaps one day the full story of the WD's will be told, and they will then receive the long overdue national gratitude which Canada owes to that truly brave band of pioneer women.

They had tremendous obstacles to overcome in the early war years. Prejudice and ignorance, in the form of whispering campaigns, swept across the country charging them with immorality. The whispers said that the women were riddled with VD, and that their illegitimate children were causing huge problems for a troubled government.

These national issues were high hurdles for girls wishing to join the services, but they paled beside the ones used by their own families and their own loved ones. Here they were told that "nice girls never join up." Only girls of easy virtue, runaways and such, joined the services. They had to overcome the prejudice of fathers and mothers, aunts and uncles, brothers and cousins, and sometimes even sisters, who had nothing but disparaging remarks to make about women in uniform. They were laughed at and ridiculed by parents who claimed that they would be nothing but "officers' comforts" and "camp followers."

While the daughter was trying desperately to defeat the lies and general cynicism, the son was idolized as soon as he donned a uniform. He became an instant hero to his family from that very moment. It was a terribly unfair situation and it scarred many of the girls so badly that they took years to convince themselves they had done the right thing by joining the RCAF. These pressures were especially hard to endure for the first few months of terrified service. Everything was so different, so strange – and everything and everyone seemed to be their master. Frightened, in a strange world, snubbed on the street when in uniform, and with nowhere to turn, including home, they served on. Slowly, ever so slowly, they won the respect to which they were entitled: first, from their male military companions; and then, finally, from the civilian population.

The whole era begs for a thorough study by sociologists. Of course, the simple, quick explanation for the general uneasiness our girls faced, was the Canada in which we lived. It slept very soundly and snugly inside its Victorian cocoon. The war was to break many habits and the moulds from which they sprang, and many long-held myths were shattered along with them. Many Canadians were given a fresh view of the world, and the high standards the girls achieved more than helped change things forever.

With the attitudes then prevailing it is not difficult to understand the frantic and often frenzied manner in which the CWAAF began in 1941. The first 150 girls who were to be the first course of airwomen were virtually hand-picked from across Canada. All required junior matriculation or better to qualify, but the emphasis was on character, character, character. Women officers from Britain were loaned to the RCAF until our own girls could be trained to help with the initial organization. But it was a Canadian woman who was chosen to lead the women's force: Kathleen O. Walker, who had grown up in Montreal.

The RCAF had taken over Havergal College on Jarvis Street in Toronto, perhaps Canada's most famous girls' finishing school. It was here that those first 150 girls were gathered to begin what was eventually to become the Women's Division of the RCAF, which served for some twenty years.

Under the stern eye and British voice of Squadron Officer Bather, the girls got their first taste of military discipline. There were many trials and tribulations in that very first course of basic training. Four times in as many weeks Squadron Officer Bather's British voice shot into my ears: "Salome, C.T., W301013 – you are on chawge." The four "cases" went something like this . . . .

The morning after reporting to the Training Depot on Jarvis Street in Toronto, I was rudely awakened by a Corporal and ordered to dress, *on the double!* I was to be paraded before the Commanding Officer. Seated on the dais of the auditorium, flanked by two Service Police types with revolvers in holsters, was Squadron Officer Bather. She was reading off the charge of insubordination, according to KR (Air), para so-and-so and subpara so-and-so. Unaccustomed to military procedure I asked, "How could I be insubordinate in my sleep? I only arrived at 3:00 A.M. and I was very rudely awakened at 6:00 A.M. to be barked at that I am on charge."

Squadron Officer Bather fixed her sharp eyes on me and snapped, "You address me as ma'am, Salome. You were assigned to upper bunk 2B and you were found sleeping in lower bunk 1B. Ah you guilty or not guilty?"

I replied, "The upper bunk was so high, *ma'am*, a trapeze artist could not have reached it."

It was the wrong thing to say. Sentence was pronounced immediately.

"Salome, we do not tolerate undue levity heah. You will proceed to the parade squaah and there you will shovel snow until 1500 hours."

During our first week we were issued with men's air force shirts. My allergy to starch manifested itself with an unbearable itch and underarm rash. I took a pair of scissors and snipped off the sleeves. When they went to the laundry I took them myself and told the Chinese laundry man to fold them so the sleeves would not show.

The following week a kit inspection was ordered, and all our government issue clothing had to be neatly and properly displayed on our bunks, according to regulations. We all stood alongside our bunks, shined and polished, breathlessly awaiting the formal inspection. Out of the fifty girls in that room my kit was the only one inspected. I figured it was Satan who made her pick up my beautifully folded shirt and shake it. I didn't know who made her turn green, then purple, over the missing sleeves.

"Salome, you are on chawge."

I was paraded to the Equipment Officer to hear the charge of Mutilation of Government Property. While I had often been blasted by Mother Superior in convent days, this was something else. I began to believe I had been caught with TNT trying to blow up the barracks. The male Squadron Leader was livid.

"Sir," I said, "why all the fuss and bother over four cotton shirts? I've offered to pay for them, and to forget the whole affair."

I still didn't know that a lowly airwoman second class doesn't talk that way to a Squadron Leader. He roared and yelled and jumped up and down and quoted great passages from KR (Air). I was fairly terrified! I can still see his downy moustache stiffen as though it had been freshly waxed when I asked why there was all the fuss . . . . That's how I got to scrub the barrack-room floors for seven days.

The transition from civilian to military life eventually became such a traumatic experience that I soon began wishing I could go home. I began spending all my waking moments thinking: *How can I get out of this outfit?* We were the first squadron of girls to be trained and we were expected to be perfect in every respect. It was this feeling of being under a microscope every second that made things so difficult.

My dilemma was how to escape without disgracing my family and my country. The only grounds for a discharge were VD, pregnancy, or compassion – none of which appealed to me. But I never stopped scheming during that first month.

One day, when I was walking past the flagpole where the Ensign was flapping in the breeze, I thought: *Here's my chance!* I whipped up a salute – a smart, Nazi salute – and proceeded on my way. Twelve seconds later I was tossed into the rear of the Black Maria by some burly Service Police and given a short ride to the CO's office.

There I got a glimpse of hell. I had, I found, committed the unpardonable crime. There was more (much more) and I was convinced by the tirade that I would now get my discharge on the spot

(if I was not shot first – which seemed a likely possibility). No such luck. I was made to walk in and out of the CO's office twenty times. Each time giving a salute. The RCAF salute.

Finally, the long month was over. Graduation day arrived, and I was stunned to find that I had led the course. The high brass from Ottawa poured into town. This was a grand occasion with full press attention. We were the first squadron of girls to pass their training – and, naturally, there was going to be a full inspection.

It seemed that we had been polishing and cleaning for days until, breathless and spotless, we finally stood for the passing-out parade. One thing I could never tolerate was someone coming too close to me. I still cannot abide it. So it was inevitable that when the Inspecting Officer craned his neck around me to check that my hair was its regulation two inches above my shirt collar, I gulped.

In horror, he shouted, "Bed bug!" The adjutant yelled "Bed bug!" to the Warrant Officer, who yelled "Bed bug!" to the Sergeant – and it seemed to float down the long inspecting line. Before I knew what was happening I was being rushed to the hospital for inspection by the Medical Officer. Salome dropped her seven veils and stood there with not enough on to flag a taxi while the medical staff examined every inch and seam of my clothing. They found nothing to confirm the "bed bug" claim.

Suddenly it occurred to me that the brown mole on the side of my neck popped out of my shirt collar whenever I gulped. In a flash it would return back to its original position. When that was explained and understood the incident became the laugh of the day.

In spite of mythical bed bugs, barracks scrubbing, snow shovelling, and penalties galore, the years I spent in the air force were the most interesting of my entire life. I was commissioned (my crime sheet having been destroyed) and from then on I behaved in a manner becoming an officer and a lady.

Well . . . there *was* that time when I was Flying Wing Adjutant and the Warrant Officer had paraded Aircraftman Second Class, De Ligne, in front of me for reprimand. De Ligne was undergoing flying training and his barracks had been found in an untidy condition during CO's inspection that morning. He was so handsome that I decided to give it to him with both barrels, so he wouldn't think I had fallen for his magnetic charm.

Later that day the CO phoned and asked me to extend a personal invitation to Prince Albert De Ligne, cousin of King Leopold of Belgium, for dinner that evening with the Belgian Ambassador. A dinner I was expected to attend. Oh, God!

*   *   *

They marched us down to lower Rockcliffe with a brisk wind blowing in our faces. Such a minute inspection at the drill hall. Such a running around. "Corporal, is my tie straight?" "Corporal, how's my tie pin?" "Corporal, do I look okay?" I'm sure that preparing for a first night performance before the royal heads of Europe could not have created more flurry and perturbation amongst actors.

We lined up in flights, marched onto the floor. Dressed, ceremonial right dress, stood at ease, at attention, at ease. Like puppets in the hands of the puppetmaster, we jerked and snapped in perfect timing. And then for hours, or so it seemed, we stood at attention while the Commanding Officer of Station Rockcliffe addressed us.

Hat bands pinched, noses itched, backs ached, garters slipped – but still we stood there unmoving. They inspected us – passing in slow procession before our wooden stares, piercing us from head to foot with their critical glances as a small group of friends and relatives watched from the edge of the hall. Then it was over. There were congratulations and there was talk of how proud our "leaders" were of us. We were told we were the best squadron to pass out of Rockcliffe. And thus the word "morale" entered our vocabularies.

After that it was back to our lecture rooms to hear the list of postings to our various courses. Each was posted according to her chosen trade. Lila, Vickie, and I all went to Toronto.

In the heart of darkness we stood and bade passionate goodbyes to our firm friends of four weeks. We laughed, perhaps even cried. We shouted and scrambled – and were finally ejected from buses at the back of the train station where we could see row on row of shining tracks; black, puffing locomotives; and our luggage, dumped unceremoniously on the platform.

We dashed to get last-minute postcards, wandered around rather aimlessly, sat on bulging suitcases. And then, finally, we were allowed on board. There was a rush to get the perfect seat, the challenge of stowing gear, and at last – we were off to Toronto!

It seemed that I could still hear the strains of the familiar song with which we'd serenaded the airmen present at the station: *The airmen thought they'd won the war but the WD's were there before!* We had succeeded.

* * *

When I was posted to my first RCAF station I was eighteen years old. I had hardly unpacked my kit bag when I was invited to a squadron party along with two other girls who were just as young and just as fresh from trade-school training.

We joined in the singsong around the piano – singing all the war-time songs – and we had a merry time. Then, while we were singing one of the songs, I suddenly realized that I didn't know the meaning of some of the words. Neither did my companions. When one girl asked what "copulation" meant the building exploded and the roof caved in.

Later, when we returned to barracks, we looked the word up in the dictionary. I shall never forget the shock of that moment.

* * *

We were stationed at Mont Joli in the winter of 1942 and were hit with the coldest winter in a century. We wore long-johns, sweaters, scarfs, double socks, and anything and everything we could layer on under our uniforms. We still froze.

One pair of girls decided to sleep together to combat the cold. They took all the blankets off one bunk, piled them on another, and crept inside. When the WD Sergeant came along on bed check and found them sleeping together she placed them on charge, claiming that they were lesbians.

The following morning the girls went to see the Senior WD officer, complaining that they didn't understand the charge. Neither of them had ever heard the word "lesbian," and they wanted an explanation. Like most of the kids, they were fresh out of schools or convents and knew little of the uglier realities of the world.

The officer dismissed the charge – and gave the Sergeant a reprimand for being overly zealous.

* * *

When I finished high school my first idea, as I contemplated the future, was to join the air force. Travel and training I knew I would receive – but I hoped for adventure and airplanes. I was crazy to fly! Being born female I realized it wouldn't be easy . . . .

The mistake I made was saying that joining the air force was the best way to get what I wanted. My father blew up in all directions. "I'd rather see you dead," he yelled at me, "than working as an officers' comfort!"

In those days I still believed that he knew what the world was all about. And a girl on the prairies didn't know if she could strike out on her own. Feeling terribly insecure I went to Normal School, instead. That was a disaster. A disaster that resulted in my joining up, anyway – but later, when I'd learned to think for myself and didn't need a parental signature.

It took a long time for father to come around. Perhaps he never understood that the job I did was little different from any city nine-to-five grind. No glamour. No adventure. Not even airplanes.

The first time I went home it was Christmas, 1943. Father's nose was still out of joint, even though I was no longer the only girl in uniform in our area. I shouldn't have gone. My reception was almost as cold as the weather, and in December the prairies can be bitter. But I was homesick – desperately homesick for the high country and open sky and home. Perhaps I thought a taste of the west would make up for the comedies of basic training.

My brief experience of home ended with me standing in the dark, looking at a car that wouldn't start, and wondering how I would catch a 5:00 A.M. eastbound train. Father hadn't done much to combat the weather. As far as he was concerned I had got myself in, and I could get myself out. So it was hike it to the depot or end up AWOL.

The distance meant little after all our route marches – but this time the temperature was sub-zero. Hindsight makes it easy to know what I should have done: pull on a parka and heavy boots, and leave them at the depot. But it was different, then. One was supposed to be in uniform, even though service shoes, lisle hose, and thin overshoes were not fit gear for sub-zero prairie nights.

In time, everything went numb. Fingers and feet and nose. They stayed numb until well after the train was on its way to Winnipeg. It wasn't much fun thawing out, but in a situation like that you don't tell anyone because you feel so stupid. No one would ever

have known – except that I couldn't get my shoes on, once I had taken them off in the barracks.

I went to the base hospital and promptly got thrown into a hospital bed. When the Medical Officer made his rounds he insinuated that I was "swinging the lead." I answered something to the effect that I didn't mind the GD work but I couldn't get my GD shoes on and I'd be only too happy to leave his GD hospital as soon as I got what I'd come for in the first place! Namely, a chit – giving me permission to wear anything I could get on my feet till they were back to normal. The look I received was not exactly friendly. But I did get the excuse.

For a week I limped to the hangar and to work in highly unorthodox footgear. The Mess hall, which was farther away from barracks, was tougher. I remember the laughter. How ridiculous to go home – where one is supposed to be cherished – and freeze one's feet.

I never went home again. Not in all the months I spent in uniform. And, even after that, never in winter.

* * *

In the early war years, women in the RCAF had clothing problems. More precisely, uniform problems. Whoever had charge of the supply system still thought in terms of dressing airmen – or perhaps it was because women came in more variations of shape and size. Whatever the reason, we had problems.

The real unlucky girls were the ones who went through their complete basic training in their civilian clothes. They spent their time yearning for a uniform that never seemed to arrive. When it did finally appear, it demanded a whole new routine. Getting accustomed to matching a collar to a shirt was the first lesson. Learning that everything must be marked (or suddenly you had a shirt with no collars or collars with no shirt) was the second. Then came learning how to chase collar studs under bunk beds, and learning how to tie a neat regulation knot in a tie, like the men. Learning how to lace your shoes (not the way you had always done it, but the air force way) and learning to buy underclothes (that you never wore, but had to have for kit inspections).

All uniforms came with regulations. It seemed queer to have pockets in a tunic and then be forbidden to carry anything in them.

But we soon learned when and how to wink at regulations. Affection grew for the old "pie-crust hat" that was superseded by more chic headgear. And some of us liked the old original pleated skirts and multi-pocketed tunics – even if we couldn't use the pockets. Moreover, some legs didn't look too bad in regulation lisle.

We often celebrated at the old Marlborough Hotel in Winnipeg, and no one paid much attention to who came with whom or, for that matter, how they behaved. There were no pubs for ladies in those days, but the laws about drinking weren't that strictly enforced. Once in a while, though, the law bestirred itself and the place was raided. Somehow, word always got there before the police and there was a tremendous rush to get dressed and get out of the hotel.

On one occasion, one couple was not fast enough. As they were passed into custody they were followed by stares and then snickers. They were wearing each other's shirt collars.

* * *

There was a pond within walking distance of our station which was used for mixed swimming parties. These were official PT outings, and were always well-chaperoned.

The airwomen were supposed to change in a wooded area to the right of a clearing, while the airmen used an area to the left. We were all busy changing one day when a great scream issued from the right side.

A WD Sergeant dashed in the direction of the scream to find two WD's half-dressed and clutching towels. "We heard someone walking just in there!" they said excitedly, pointing into the bush.

The female Sergeant gathered herself and, in a stern, authoritative voice declared, "All right! Whoever you are come out of there immediately. We know you're there. Come out at once!"

We all clustered around staring at the spot in the trees. Suddenly there was a rustle and a long "Moo!" as a cow wandered from the bush.

* * *

We were stationed across from the United States Air Force base at Fort Pepperell, St. John's, Newfoundland. It was the official home base for RCAF personnel attached to No. 1 Group Headquarters. Since this was years before Newfoundland joined the Canadian Confederation, being stationed there was classified as serving overseas. The camp was opened in August 1943, and for several weeks there were no fences around our air force reserve. We would emerge from barracks in the morning to find cows ambling about – and we learned to tread with the utmost care!

At one particular softball game between airmen and airwomen an officer rounded third base and headed for home, only to slip on a strategically placed "cow flap." He slid all the way to home plate picking up more than mud on his official blue uniform pants. A few innings later, an entire herd of cows ambled onto the outfield and brought the game to a halt. Some of the airwomen who had never been outside a city in their lives departed the ball field "on the double."

Another time we were holding a bonfire and shore supper at Long's Pond, which was in walking distance of our camp. Some of the airwomen had taken blankets from their cots and brought them to spread on the sand. When we arrived back at barracks after a great evening one girl found her blanket emitting a strange but strong odour. She had managed to lay it directly on top of a "pancake." She had some difficulty explaining the soiled blanket to the Equipment Officer on the following Monday.

* * *

When we first began flying C-130 Hercules aircraft in the RCAF we were continually embarrassed by having to refuse to fly airwomen. The manufacturers hadn't thought about women when they designed the C-130. The only toilet, a rather majestic chemical affair, sat totally exposed at the rear of the aircraft.

I was scheduled to fly from Trenton to Edmonton, and they wanted to load a bunch of young WD's who were headed for the Supply Depot at Namao. The Air Movements Unit refused to load them. Somehow, the Air Officer Commanding got wind of this and charged into action, as only he could do. He insisted that military aircraft could carry all personnel.

"You can solve the problem any way you like!" he stormed. "But those girls are going aboard."

Luckily I was rescued by my navigator. He stepped forward, most gallantly, and warned the girls of the lack of toilet facilities.

"Please," he pleaded, "make an effort to go before you get on board."

* * *

One cold winter's day in 1944, just a few days before Christmas, the US Navy invited twenty-five of our airwomen from Torbay to an afternoon party at their base in Argentia.

We drove over in a bus in the beginnings of a major Newfie snowstorm. As the party progressed, so did the gale, and ultimately we were stranded and had to remain overnight. We were put up in a spare ward of the hospital where the accommodations were great for sleeping. Very comfortable cots. But when we entered the washroom we found six urinals and one toilet – for twenty-five women!

After some discussion, an orderly arrived with a supply of bedpans and things settled down. It wasn't long, however, before one of the girls wanted to carry her bedpan to the washroom. She came running back to announce that there was a Shore Patrol stationed on guard at the door of our ward. The washroom was located in the hallway.

After hearing that, nobody had the nerve to go out into the hall carrying a bedpan. As we all sat there, wondering what to do, one airwoman had a brainwave. "We'll just dump the pans out the window!" she declared triumphantly.

We did just that. But the next morning, when we lined up to board our bus, we were embarrassed to see a brilliant yellow patch of snow directly beneath our ward window.

* * *

We were all confined to barracks at Havergal Trade School to prepare for Commanding Officer's inspection. Everything had to be scrubbed from top to bottom and we were all busy as bees, washing and cleaning. Florrie was washing the windows using a Kotex pad as a polisher. (We used to use them as shoe brushes, too. They made terrific polishing pads.) In her industrious activity she inadvertently dropped her pad out the window. It fell just beside the guard house at the main entrance.

We had to get that pad back at all costs – but we couldn't figure out how to go about it. We could hardly explain to the guard that we were "just going outside to pick up a sanitary pad." I think it was Scottie who saved the day. She dropped her brush out the window and said, "There. All you have to do is go downstairs and tell the guard you have to retrieve your brush."

Of course, we retrieved the other evidence as well.

* * *

When I returned to barracks one Sunday evening after spending a weekend pass in town, I underwent the usual routine of removing every vestige of civilian life. Since I had painted my fingernails a deep pink for a Saturday night dance, these unmilitary traces were my first concern . . . .

I spent every evening for the next week in the Mess kitchen, with my arms up to the elbows in dishwater. During Monday morning's parade the Squadron Officer had had no difficulty in noticing that I'd forgotten to remove the polish from the pinky of my right hand.

* * *

When you consider that RCAF stations were like small towns – with their work and recreation areas, housing, fire-stations, offices, hangars, maintenance units, and all the rest – the crime rate was surprisingly low. The small air force police detachment usually had an easy time maintaining law and order.

At one station I commanded in the 1960s we had an air force policewoman in our detachment. This girl was a real asset; friendly and efficient, she could handle just about any situation. I say "just about" any problem – for I remember one occasion when she got rather upset. These were the facts reported to me.

Late one night, as she was entering the airwomen's quarters, she encountered a couple just inside the entrance who were locked in a sexual embrace usually referred to as a "knee trembler." Rather shocked at this spectacle she shouted, "Stop that immediately!"

This was met with a snarling, "Fuck off."

Our girl was having none of that insolence. With more emphasis she declared, "You stop that at once! I'm a policewoman."

The highly agitated male voice came back with, "I don't care who you are – I'm an officer – so fuck off you Dickless Tracy!"

*   *   *

We had a WD Sergeant on our base who worked for the Commanding Officer. She was a lot older than most of the airwomen and older than many of the male officers. She got away with murder because even the Old Man was afraid to lock horns with her. She always remained on duty in the CO's office until ten o'clock each evening. Not that it was required . . . she was just fearful that an important call might come through and no one would answer it. After preparing herself for bed, she would don her pyjamas and kimono, pick up her knitting, and trot across the road to the Administration Building. She did this on each and every evening. It was easy to see that she thought the weight of the war rested solely on her shoulders.

On one particularly stormy night she was curled up in her big chair, knitting needles flashing, when she heard the door to the outside office open. In trotted "Wingey," the station mascot. The wire-haired terrier was shaking and tossing water in all directions.

"Who is the half-brained nitwit who would take you for a walk on a night like this?" she bellowed.

"I suppose I'm the half-brained nitwit, Sergeant," said the CO, coming through the door. "But you're a bigger one! What in God's name are you doing in here dressed like that? Pick up your knitting and get back to your barracks – *on the double!*"

We could hardly believe the old girl would tell the story on herself. She was one scrappy old bag.

*   *   *

When the WD barracks burned down at No. 16 Service Flying Training School, Hagersville, the fire was attributed to faulty wiring. Fortunately, there were no casualties; but there was concern that some shift workers, who were sleeping at the time, might not have escaped.

We were all clustered around as the firemen fought the blaze when a WD appeared at the upstairs door leading to the safety escape slide. She was clad in her pyjamas and stood there, hesitating, as we all urged her to slide down. Suddenly she turned and disappeared into the burning building and a great cry arose from the bystanders.

Several minutes passed before she reappeared – and then she was carrying two pillows! Stepping out the door she daintily placed these on the escape slide, seated herself on top of them, and proceeded to make a majestic escape.

*　*　*

On the morning that we received our medical discharge from the RCAF we had to get in line and collect a bottle from an orderly sitting behind a desk. The line was a longish one, and to my horror it was ladies and gentlemen mixed. This was extremely embarrassing for me, and was made even more so when I caught sight of an officer I knew.

I was so unnerved that when I got my bottle I made a dive for the nearest lavatory – and found myself in a men's washroom with three toilets in a row. Bolting into one of these I discovered that the partitions didn't go right to the floor. And next to me I could see the trousers of an airman!

I was so shattered by this time that I missed the bottle. I was almost too mortified to come out of the cubicle. Then, when I handed the bottle (containing only a drop) to the orderly, he told me, "Sorry. You'll have to do better than that."

In a high state of shock I managed to find the women's washroom on the next go-round. But it upset me for days.

*　*　*

The most memorable Christmas I spent during the war happened in 1943. For some unknown reason I was the only WD on strength at No. 5 Equipment Depot in Moncton. Perhaps that accounted for why I escaped unscathed after being AWOL for a week from my Christmas leave.

I had decided that I would try to find a cousin who had married a member of the Royal Canadian Mounted Police and was living in North Ingonish, near the top of Cape Breton Island. I had forgotten her married name but reasoned that there would be little trouble finding the Mountie's home in North Ingonish, which was doubtless a small place.

It was the day before Christmas, and I arrived at North Sydney by train, expecting to take a bus up the coast to my destination. The first setback came when I learned that the coastal highway was snowbound and buses weren't running. The second setback came when I was told that the Mountie at North Ingonish was an old chap who was not married. I decided it didn't really matter if that were true or not as I couldn't get there, anyway. So off to the local hotel I trudged to seek a night's lodging before catching the train back to Moncton.

The hotel was a pleasant surprise: very old world and very warm and friendly. I was soon welcomed into a group of young people enjoying a few pints at the bar. It developed that they, too, were bound for points north and didn't intend to let a bit of snow keep them from getting home for Christmas. They suggested I join them in their old Lizzie, guaranteed to make it through any snowstorm. Why not, indeed?

Things weren't too bad for several miles but the farther we went the worse became the drifts. Several times we successfully pushed Lizzie out of deep snow. Then dusk descended. We were still far from our destinations and were climbing Old Smokey, which got steeper and steeper. At last it happened. Old Lizzie not only refused to budge, she also refused to cough when we tried to coax her into starting. There was nothing in sight but snow, pine trees, and twinkling stars. And nothing to do but walk.

That Christmas Eve walk is the most memorable of my life. It wasn't particularly cold. The stars, huge and brilliant globes, hung in the sky and reflected off the pristine snow. Eventually the moon came up and lighted our way; and once we had our second wind, even the uphill climb didn't seem too arduous.

Just the same we were delighted, some hours later, to catch a glimpse of light ahead. We crowded eagerly into the warmth of the little farmhouse kitchen. Hot, weak cocoa, stale biscuits, and hard benches – all a very marvellous and welcome part of our adventure. By this time, it was revealed, we were less than twenty miles from North Ingonish.

Negotiations and the passing of a hat produced a sleigh, a team of horses, and a driver. A team of horses equipped, no less, with a set of sleigh bells. We sang every Christmas carol ever written as we perched on our beautiful sled and jingled our way into North Ingonish, right up to the door of the local Mountie's house. I was tremendously relieved when my cousin's face popped up behind the large male figure who answered our insistent knocking.

Over the all too short days of my Christmas leave I skiied, skated, and "first footed," giving little attention to my return journey. Why worry? The buses were running again. Or at least they did – until the day I was due to go south. Then there was another wild snowstorm.

Eventually, the Mountie managed to get me aboard a little local steamer that was heading for Sydney. The boat rolled and tossed and threatened to sink permanently under the huge waves, but it got us there safely. By great luck, I was in time to catch the train for Moncton.

When I appeared back at camp my Flight Sergeant, after listening to my story, suggested that I was some kind of nut. But he was content to overlook my seven days absence without leave.

*   *   *

Why did I enlist in the WD's? I'm sure it was the thrill of adventure – a way out. I was eighteen years old, the eldest daughter in a rural parson's family of two sons and four daughters, and I had only known small town life.

My eldest brother was already enlisted in the army – my boyfriend in the air force. I think my Dad was great about my own decision. In those days, country folk looked on women in the service as "for the use of the men." But Dad let me go. I wonder what I would have done if he hadn't?

I was classified as a clerk accountant – I suppose because I had taken a business course and was working in an insurance office. After entry at Rockcliffe I went to Trenton for training. It was a time of much experience . . . .

The agonizing days in class when everyone had dysentery – would I last until free to get to the latrine? Marching in platoons – you never just walked anywhere. Making a date with an airman across the table in the Mess – then forgetting what he looked like (or only remembering what he looked like from the waist up). Racing the airmen to the post office. And then there was the time when I was relaxing on my top bunk on a warm summer's evening in my underwear. I felt an odd sensation, and looking up and across to the men's barracks I saw field glasses pointed at me!

At Trenton I asked to be posted "as far as I could go." Which was, it turned out, Vancouver. Oh, the wonderful train ride! I remember poking my head out of the curtains of my upper bunk to ask a passerby, "Do you have the time?" "Yes," came the answer, "do you have the inclination?" Gulp. A fast retreat into my bunk.

Now things began to move quickly. First I was switched to equipment accounting (instead of pay records, which I liked better). Then I was posted to Pat Bay, on loan to the RAF; and after that, Comox (3,000 men and thirty women – great for the ego). Next it was overseas to London, and back to pay accounts. I used to look up to watch the bomber raids going out, and think that the crews were so young. And I would go to the military hospitals to see people from home for my Dad. I shared a wonderful apartment in Earl's Court with two WD's. Both house-mates got married, and held their receptions there.

By the time VE Day arrived, I had been promoted to Corporal. It was a hot, muggy day, and it didn't seem right to celebrate. Too many friends were gone for good. Then we looked out the window – and there was my brother! A Lieutenant! He'd fought his way through North Africa, Italy, and across the Continent to England. I hadn't seen him since 1942. What a party we had! It was the first time I ever passed out drunk – but I admit he beat me to it!

It was a marvellous experience. I wonder what I would have done with my life otherwise?

Grounded

When my skipper, Mike Humphrey, first reported to 408 Squadron he had a unique introduction. Mike was an American kid serving with the RCAF and a Sergeant at the time of the incident.

He had been told to report at 0900 hours and he biked to the hangar, punctual to the minute. There was no one in the office at B Flight when he arrived, so he ambled out into the hangar. The hangars at Linton-on-Ouse were fitted with overhead chain blocks for lifting engines, gun turrets, and props. Two sets of chains dangled down from the ceiling. One set to raise and lower the large hook and the other to move the hoist along its overhead track.

Mike busied himself that morning by lowering the hook, placing it under the crossbar of his bike, then lifting the bike up to the hangar ceiling. Next he began carefully sliding the hoist along its track the length of the hangar. As Mike approached the end of the hangar he noticed that he was no longer alone. A jeep had driven in while he was engrossed in lifting his bike, and a Squadron Leader was drumming his fingers on its front fender with a "what the hell have we here" look on his face. Mike hastily lowered his bike, unhooked it, jumped on, and peddled away without any exchange of words.

When he reported to B Flight about half an hour later, his hand was in the middle of his salute before he noticed that he was saluting the Squadron Leader he had seen with the jeep.

* * *

My fellow airwoman, Myrna, and I travelled on that famous tub, the *Lord Rodney*, to our posting at No. 1 Group Headquarters at St. John's. Because our ship was dodging subs (or so the more imaginative allowed), the trip was a long, roundabout one. This gave us the opportunity to make the acquaintance of several of the Newfie civilians on board. Including one, John by name, a very debonair man-about-St.-John's. He pursued his friendship with the WAAF's – as he insisted on calling us – after we were ensconced at Kenna's Hill Barracks, just outside St. John's.

One day, as we were being marched from barracks to our offices in the city, John suddenly appeared alongside driving a jeep. By ill fate, Myrna and I were marching on the inner flank of the parade, nearest to him and his car. When he first invited us to hop in we ignored him and kept on marching. Then the Sergeant, who had noticed the invitation, let out a stentorian roar: "Any WD who puts one foot inside that jeep is on charge!" Who could resist a challenge like that? Certainly not Myrna and I.

The Sergeant was as good as his word. We spent the next fourteen days scrubbing the guard house floors.

Several times during my fifteen-month tour of duty at No. 1 Group Headquarters, my boss, who was a Wing Commander, mused aloud over the possible reasons why, after his strong recommendations, I had not been given stripes.

I hadn't the heart to give him the details of one possibly very strong reason.

* * *

Anyone who served with the RCAF at Gander, Newfoundland, will remember the weather – particularly the tremendous winds. It was pretty grim, sometimes, for girls trying to buck that wind. I remember trying to get from the recreation hall to the Mess in one of those sixty-miles-an-hour gales. I'm not very big, and the wind kept picking me up and blowing me over. After about three or four tumbles I had just about decided to give up and go back to the rec-hall when a mountain of a man who worked in the Motor Transport Section came along, swept me up in his arms, and carried me bodily. I can't even remember his name, today, but I was ever so thankful. I guess it looked pretty ridiculous to those watching – but I didn't mind.

* * *

Late one night, after a large, beery evening, I was escorting a WAAF Officer home to her quarters. We were riding our bicycles, single-file in the blackout, when we came to a rather steep hill.

The route to the WAAF barracks was down the hill, which had a very sharp turn at the bottom. This was no problem under normal conditions. But tonight, after failing to negotiate the turn as the WAAF had done, I plunged into a ditch. I struck my head on something and was stunned for a time. I fully expected the WAAF to come to my rescue.

Evidently, though, she had gone her merry way. When I awoke some three hours later I was still in the ditch. I staggered back to barracks with a splitting headache.

* * *

There should be an RCAF bicycle museum, or at least a memorial, erected to those trusty steeds that gave such yeoman service during the war. With the polluted and traffic-choked roads of the present day, it's nice to remember when we sailed along on our bikes, carefree and utterly independent.

Cycling around the airbase, whether it was to dispersal or to the Messes, provided both exercise and an opportunity to escape and relax. Some bicycles seemed to know their way, day or night, to your favourite pub. Others wouldn't behave unless they were escorting bicycles of the opposite sex down a country lane.

It's a wonder they ever behaved at all after the rough banging and pounding they endured from their careless and often deceitful owners. They would be left defenceless, leaning against any vertical object, be it pub, garden wall, haystack, tree, or cottage door. Here they could be leaped upon by others and driven off hurriedly into the night, spending the rest of their days covered in mud and seemingly abandoned under the eaves of wayside inns.

My own iron steed was purchased, sight unseen, over a pub table one merry night. Its owner was being repatriated to Canada and needed the ten dollars to continue his revelry. In the morning I learned from a quick, walk-around inspection that the deal had been one sided. The rear wheel had several kinks that gave the bike a lurching motion, and it tracked up the road like a dog on a summer day. The frame was bent, requiring the rider to lean to the left to counter-balance a list to starboard. Too late – my ten dollars was halfway to Canada!

Making allowances for alignment and learning to correct for track error took a little time, but eventually I became the master. One of my bike's built-in assets was protection against theft, since no one else could ride it. On one evening, I left the Mess just in time to see my bike leaving under the inebriated guidance of a squadron mate. He quickly discovered that his hands didn't line up with the rest of his anatomy . . . . By the time I reached the scene of the crash he was crawling along the ditch, leaking blood.

I covered many happy and carefree miles on my trusty steed – and no matter where I parked it, day or night, it was always waiting to take me home. We parted only on the morning the squadron left Down Ampney for India.

After takeoff I flew across the village and over the house where I had boarded. There, from her garden, our devoted landlady extended a final farewell wave. And there, leaning against the wall where I had placed it the previous night, rested my faithful steed.

I have never returned to Down Ampney, but during the 1960s my navigator spent a couple of weeks each summer in that area. He always used my bike for transportation. I'm sure that if I were to go back today, my old ten-dollar purchase would still be there, leaning against a tree or hedge. There would be no chains or locks restraining it. It would never condone that kind of treatment.

* * *

I was in No. 1 Fighter Wing when it transferred from North Luffenham in England to Marville in France, early in 1955. Everyone's first priority was finding wheels, since there were no married quarters and our families were scattered about – mostly in neighbouring Belgium. We provided a bonanza for numerous car salesmen, who began to surface ten minutes after the Roundel reached the top of the flagpole.

Citroën, Mercedes, Opel, Volkswagen, Simca, and Vauxhall were just a few of the brands available. What to buy was a problem. My dilemma was solved by a friend who worked in the Mobile Equipment Section. He was continually singing the praises of his little 1955 Simca. All Simcas of that era were painted a very dark green which I didn't find unattractive. After much mental debate that took my friend's automotive know-how into consideration, I decided to place an order for a new Simca and duly deposited $1,320.

The waiting period for delivery was several weeks, but eventually it arrived spic and span. My friend in the ME section was away on Temporary Duty when my car arrived, and almost a month elapsed before I met him again. We were in the operations room, and after the usual greetings things got around to cars and engines. My friend had learned some new things about carburettors and fuel systems while away on course, and he was full of exuberance about these new discoveries. "Come on, I'll show you what I mean!" he said.

I followed him outside and along a line of parked cars until we reached a dark green Simca, and there he rather unceremoniously jerked up the hood and dived inside. Off came the air breather and hoses, then the distributor cap, and within five minutes the engine workings were exposed. All the time I was listening to a rapid-fire dissertation on fuel efficiency. By the time my friend had divulged all his findings, delivered his lecture, replaced the parts, and stood back, he had completed a fairly acceptable tune-up.

Dusting himself off he slammed down the hood with a resounding crash and we stood there, leaning on the car and chatting. Suddenly my friend asked, "Where did you get those side-view mirrors?" I looked at the set of twin mirrors – and sensing that something was amiss by my delay in answering he hastily said, "Isn't this your car?" To which I could only reply: "No. Isn't it yours?"

Our conversation was resumed about six blocks away.

The vehicle we had just serviced belonged to the Chief Operations Officer. It was parked directly beneath his window, less than six feet from his desk.

*　　*　　*

I have owned many cars of many makes and models over the years, but my all-time favourite is a 1950 Citroën. I bought it when I was posted to France to join the Air Division.

It was already ten years old when I fell in love with its huge fenders. Thicker than any Model T's, those fenders swept upwards in large, curving arcs. Even the tiny, underpowered engine of eleven horsepower and four cylinders mesmerized me. That particular make of Citroën was named for its horsepower: a Citroën "Onze."

Over the years nearly everyone has had something go wrong with their car. I am no exception to the rule – but I learned a unique one with the Onze. Filled to the brim with *essence* the old Citroën was supposedly good for 250 kilometres. When I ran out of gas one day, only an hour after filling the tank, I was positive I had a leaking tank or gas line. Sitting on a lovely French road in the summer sun, I tried to analyze the problem. *Must* be a leak, I concluded. I took some newspapers out of the trunk, placed them under the gas tank, and waited. Not a drop fell. I spread the papers under the engine. Nothing. Then I placed the papers the length of the car, under the gas line. Not one drop hit the paper. I crawled under and examined the bottom of the gas tank. No sign of damage. No hole. Dry as a bone.

A friendly soul gave me a lift to a gas station and dropped me back at the Onze with a can of gas. I proceeded to pour the gas into the tank but it would take only a few litres before overflowing. Starting the car, I drove straight home. While I wanted to find and fix the trouble I was not, with my limited ability in French, anxious to tackle those formidable French mechanics. I persisted with the Jerry can. It became an indispensable part of the Onze.

Of course, the car was painted black. I doubt if there was any other colour used in France when my Citroën rolled from the factory. Perhaps it was a throwback to Henry Ford's famous dictum. It had as much room as a station wagon and our four young children roamed its interior with great glee. Sitting in the back placed them five feet behind the driver. And they especially loved the jump seats.

With rack-and-pinion steering and front-wheel drive the Citroën steered like a sports car, handling the sharp, ninety degree bends of those tree-lined French roads with magnificent ease. It was as heavy as a tank, and its long wheel base and wide track made it more suitable for an ambulance, but it had romance written all over it.

Every movie that I have ever seen starring Rex Harrison has him driving an old Citroën. Raincoat collar up, hat down. Eyes peering through a rain-streaked windshield, watching for hairpin curves. A quick whip around them with headlight beams dancing off wet cobblestones . . . . Mystery, intrigue, romance – but alas, French engineering.

Someone has written that a good definition of hell is a place where the Americans are the lovers, the Germans the police, the British the cooks, and the French the mechanics. I tend to agree, especially with the last classification. Each and every mechanical breakdown was traumatic and the Onze and I became sad but familiar objects to every mechanic in the town of Metz.

To start with, the car was underpowered for its great size and weight. Although it may have done 120 kilometres an hour when new, the best I could coax from its tiny engine was 100 kilometres. Not that this dissatisfied me. With young children riding inside, sixty was adequate; and it gave a feeling of safety. Still, a little more power for those long hills and for passing in tight situations would have been useful.

It might have been easier to effect repairs had I been fluent in the French language. But that is debatable, since all the mechanics had switched their loyalty to the new Citroën – the totally redesigned model. (The thing could pump itself up and down hydraulically and had a shape only a Frenchman could love.)

When the Onze and I appeared in their midst the mechanics gathered around more from a sense of curiosity than from an interest in working on it. They would thump its great fenders with rubber hammers and cry, "*Ancienne!*" "*Antique!*" and "*Regardez l'aile avant!*" (which I think meant the fenders). But they never understood what I wanted fixed.

When the transmission in the Onze ground to a halt I had the car towed into the nearest garage, which also happened to be the largest in the city of Metz. I failed completely to relate the nature of the malfunction although I tried with every mechanic I could collar. In desperation I searched our RCAF base for a French Canadian who understood cars. I finally found a Corporal who worked in the Motor Pool and we struck a bargain. He accompanied me to the garage to explain, in expert French, that the transmission was broken. But we failed (or rather he did) to convey the remotest idea of the problem to the puzzled mechanics.

Le transmission was the term he used, over and over – except he said it with a decided flavouring of French. While it failed to communicate the problem it did give me an insight into the language spoken by French Canadians in those days. They used hundreds of English words spoken with Gallic intonations in place of actual French words. *Le spark plug*, for instance. I found it didn't mean anything to a French mechanic.

It turned out that the dictionary had the words I needed for transmission. *Boîte de vitesses*. Speed box. Exactly. How simple, how clever.

It wasn't until I made a trip to the Luxembourg airport to pick up a friend that I got caught without the Jerry can on board. We were returning over the Luxembourg-French border when the Onze died. Already suffering some anxiety over the expensive pottery he had purchased in Holland, the last thing my friend wanted was an inquisition by Customs. We had been waved through the Luxembourg Customs without stopping and had travelled halfway to the French barrier when the Onze stopped.

"What the hell is the matter?" my friend asked nervously. We

could see the French Customs officers taking their ease against their barrier.

"Out of gas, I guess."

"Out of gas?" he yelped. "But you filled up in Luxembourg!"

"Well, this old girl is queer," I replied. "The tank goes dry after an hour. Relax, there's a gas station here at the border."

As we climbed out we were met by the Luxembourg and French Customs officials who had marched up to inquire about our problem. We were in no-man's-land. My friend threw his coat over his suitcase in the back seat, while I said something brilliant in French like, "*Sans essence.*" Luckily, this sufficed to explain our stopping. With great good humour they all pitched in and pushed the Onze over the border. No Customs inspection, no questions, no showing of papers.

After that episode I bought another Jerry can, and from then on two were always strapped into the trunk. Not that it did any good since one can was more than sufficient. But it seemed the prudent thing to do.

Family trips through Germany in the Onze were always embarrassing for the children. The German drivers in their shiny Mercedes boomed past us on the Autobahn. Not content to pass they all leaned out laughing, pointing at the Onze cruising along at a sedate ninety kilometres. I couldn't hear the German words flung in our direction but I could tell by the laughter that they must be derogatory. It upset the children, who asked questions about the merriment we were causing – questions I turned aside by suggesting that the Germans were simply jealous of our classic automobile.

We were often able to turn the tables on them in the winter. Two inches of snow left them spinning their rear wheels while the front-wheel drive Citroën sailed past with majestic ease. And a smiling driver.

The Onze was side-swiped by a new Mercedes one day as I wound through the streets of Munich. Luckily, I had the right of way – but the noise of ripping metal made my heart leap. I descended from the driver's seat to examine my pride and joy. Not a scratch. Not a dent. Not a fleck of paint missing. Satisfied, I turned to the German who was inspecting his new car. It was ripped open from front to back with chrome trim hanging like tinsel from a tree.

One should never gloat. We all know that. But there are times. I motored on. The Onze undefeated. Its driver in sublime good humour.

The French, like the British, build their cars for tropical climates; or they did in those days. The instrument inserted as a heater may have worked in a Florida summer, but in France it failed to take fog off the windshield. Perhaps that was why the windshield could be swung open in a horizontal forward action. This allowed for good visibility, although it was hard on the nose in winter.

Touring in France, in any season, required careful planning. All of the children were well-toileted prior to embarkation. Finding an oasis for relief was difficult, if not impossible. Unless you bought *essence* or *huile* the gas stations ruled their facilities out-of-bounds. This quid pro quo system of exchange sometimes stretched things to the limit. We took along a chamber pot that could be used onboard the Onze. While there was plenty of room to manoeuvre the pot in the back seat, we often (usually in a traffic jam) over-estimated the holding capacity of the smaller boys. The confusion, and the distaff protests, added an extra fillip to any long-range journey.

We had learned, from the beginning, that roadside bushes were the only avenue open on most occasions. Cars constantly screeched to a halt in front of you. Doors would be flung open as bodies tumbled out and streaked for cover. Our children would laugh and chant, "We know where you're going, we know where you're going." While I laughed with them I also made mental calculations of gas consumption, soft drink consumption, miles travelled, and the likelihood of a decent restaurant appearing. If the computation was wrong we, too, were forced into the weeds.

One day, travelling on a main highway, I watched a succession of cars pull up abruptly, their passengers scrambling out for relief. Each time I was forced to wait until the oncoming traffic cleared before pulling around the empty car. (The drivers never bothered to pull onto the shoulder of the road. They simply applied the brakes and departed.) Creeping cautiously around one empty car, thinking that the occupants were all absorbed elsewhere, I was surprised to find a man and woman seated at a card table placed directly in front of their vehicle. They were enjoying lunch, complete with the necessary bottle of wine. *Vive la France! Vive la différence!*

Spare parts for the Onze were never a problem. The countryside seemed littered with old Citroëns put out to pasture. My only ongoing problem was the gas tank. It wasn't until the air force transferred me home, and I reluctantly put the Onze up for sale, that the mystery of the gas tank was solved.

With a one hundred dollar price tag the Onze received attention from a number of tire-kickers. The buyer, it turned out, was another car nut (buff). I saw the particular gleam in his eye that only a bona fide second-hand car buyer recognizes. He was hooked as soon as he ran his hands over those beautiful thick fenders.

I explained the gas tank situation with some trepidation – after the hundred dollars was folded neatly into my wallet. The buyer never turned a hair.

"Oh, I think I know what the problem is!" he said, to my amazement. "It's probably a collapsed gas tank." He got down on his knees and felt under the bumper and along the top of the gas tank. "Sure, look, feel here," he directed me. "The top of the tank has collapsed downwards. That's why it wouldn't hold more than a few litres at a time. Simple. I can fix that."

I knelt beside him, feeling the top of the tank, remembering all those refills from the Jerry can over the past four years.

Au revoir, Onze. Bon voyage!

* * *

We had an airframe mechanic stationed with our crew in Yorkshire, on 434 Squadron. His passion was beating the British railroads. No effort was too great to avoid paying his train fare. It wasn't through cheapness. It had absolutely nothing to do with money, in the larger sense. It was a game, much like beating the pay telephones. I guess it's called beating the system.

This guy had a wallet full of railroad platform tickets. Remember? You needed a ticket to get onto the station platform. Your ticket to ride the train was the responsibility of the train conductor or, more often, the agent at the station where you arrived.

Many times, I watched Jack jump over the barricade at York

station when the ticket-taker's attention was diverted. On a longer trip to Leeds, for example, he would buy a train ticket to the first station on the line and ride right into Leeds city station using a platform ticket from his collection. It was unbelievable, the amount of pleasure he got from beating the system! After every trip he would gleefully recount his latest coup to us in minute detail.

One night I made the mistake of arriving at Leeds station with him. I began walking for the gate when I was grabbed by Jack. "No, no!" he hissed. "You're going the wrong way."

He headed us back along the train tracks about a quarter of a mile. Here we had to climb up a steep embankment, slipping and sliding in the mud. Then at the top we had to climb a fairly high brick wall that faced the tracks. This landed us in the dirty yards of a factory – and we had to climb out of *this* on the other end. Eventually, we arrived back at the city square, filthy but victorious.

It took a half hour in a wash-and-brush-up shop before we could start our forty-eight hour pass. But the important thing was that we had beaten the system. And beaten the railroad out of a couple of shillings.

* * *

In the late 1940s, we had an Engineering Officer on 408 Squadron whom I have never forgotten. Although he was only a Flying Officer he was solely responsible for a large gaggle of Lancasters. We airmen all looked up to him and gave him our total support. Mainly, I suppose, because he looked after us and was such a decent person.

When our annual thirty days leave rolled around, he always allowed everyone to claim Vancouver as their leave address – which meant tacking on eight days travelling time from Ottawa. He did other things for us, too, and we were always looking for ways to pay him back.

In the spring of 1949 he went off on a site inspection tour of northern photo bases. He had hardly cleared the end of the runway before the airmen gathered in the hangar to discuss a little project we had talked about previously. The Flying Officer drove a very rusty and banged-up old 1938 Chev, and he had parked it alongside the hangar before flying off. We pulled it into the back of the hangar where it would be out of the way and started in on it.

We began by re-upholstering the interior. Then we did an engine job while another crew knocked out the dents and filled the holes in the body. When we had the engine and trunk cleaned and the bumpers straightened we painted the whole car blue. A colour that just matched the blue in our aircrafts' roundels.

When the officer returned to the squadron, we all made sure to be on hand. We were all skulking around various corners, keeping an eye on the parking lot. Going over to the row of cars the Engineering Officer walked up and down a few times, scratching his head. Then he came back into the hangar complaining that his car was gone. He was told to go and check the licence plates . . . .

Later, he came around to thank each of us personally. And a few nights later he got everyone into the Wet canteen and bought a whole bunch of beer.

Poetically Speaking

BIOGRAPHY

Tom Farley

The trips that made your tour you filed concisely
In dog-eared log, and, as became a chap
Who battled, you took the honours rather nicely
And wore them in the angle of your cap,
Less than a thought. And less than thought to you
Were all the lines John Keats or Shelley said;
No skylark, roared your bomber in the blue;
No *belle dame sans merci* sang in your head.

Mendicant never, you paid your way in full,
Laughed in your ale and sought no man's light praises.
Twenty trips out, where deadly beautiful
The bombing run left little time for phrases,
You prang'd the target, cursed the English showers,
And down the road, beyond the "Lion's Head"
Shared with a WAAF two moonlit haystack hours
Till turning props dispersed the words you said.

What did you say, who watched the red moon rise
And flares hang in the sky above Berlin?
I'll give you this – you were too big for lies
When you spun in.

IT WAS A 'PLANE

Tom Farley

It was a 'plane adrift beneath the moon
upon a sea of clouds; it slid through beams
serenely as an angel of the night,
faint as a song,
aloof from mortal dreams.

Now Navigator,
scribe, compassing the starry tides of flight,
bowing to candid estimate of lives
and tracks-made-good upon a squared mercator,
what is your destiny in dead reckoning?
Will you make base tonight,
mission completed, or will these arrowed lines
run without intersection off the page
to pinpoint past the aerodrome of day
on the unknown, unfathomed ETA?

Aldebaran looks down upon your course
and mortal ways, immortally unconcerned
whether this night, the target prang'd, you make
your homeward journey safe; and you, back turned,
balance the abstract verities of wind and drift,
log how a city burned.

On astral tides adrift beneath the moon
there beat three lives within the engines' song,
measured in failing fuel, minutes of flight,
dreams on a wireless
a code-word long.

Hello! Hello!
Land's End Observer Corps?
We have a craft last heard from in distress
bearing your way with seven minutes' fuel,
losing height slowly, instruments gone U/S.

Green Charlie from . . . hello . . . yes, series of red
fired the minute they see land ahead.
Keep in close touch with
– Damn!
the line's gone dead.

It was a song that slipped beneath the moon
upon a sea of clouds; it slid through beams
serenely as an angel of the night,
faint as a star
aloof from mortal dreams.

DAWN SWEEP

Tom Farley

I met him on the tarmac in the dawn
(Soar again, Johnny, into the wild blue yonder!)
And he spoke to me as he buckled his harness on,
And the sky was a green glass dome with a hint of thunder:
  "It's only a split snap-second that lies between 'fire' and 'break,'
  But it's big as forever. You fire, break sharp, and the rest
  Is the luck of your cards and turns on the chances you take
  When you hit for the deck at low level and head for the west.
  O, I've hung my hat on the weeping willow tree
  And can
  No longer stay with you. So long, brother!
  I can no longer stay with you."

There is a wind that blows too loud and keen,
Swift in its rising, fatal in its fall.
Hand in your name and regimental number!
(Immortal light immobilizing dawn.)
"B" flight stand by for takeoff! Man your planes!
Run like a schoolkid gaming on the lawn.
Swimming in daylight, westward rising like thunder,
Black-bellied Mustangs, turning above the 'drome,
Immortal gyre turning.

                    Immobilized
I see two crewmen running from the Mess
To bicycles, yet they are motionless
Airmen at reveille, stricken in attitudes
Of frozen dawn whose ice hold will not die
Till Johnny's squadron drifts in from the sky.

Johnny in your bright mae west,
Johnny with your chute snapped on,
Johnny with your coupe-top back.
Where do you fly,
American Mustangs, hitting the wind for France?

Two crewmen running in a timeless trance,
The eye's bright souvenir.

                            Dead minutes pass
The WAAF at the wireless, calm as a telephone girl,
Calls with polite professional unconcern:
   "Hello, Red Leader. Hold your heading. Over!"
'Planes hang in space, waiting for earth to turn
And flash their target. Voice as sweet as clover:
   "Hello, Red Leader. This is Flower Two.
   Return to base. Return to base."

                       A few
Stray wisps of hair fall over her pale eyes,
Blue as the skies, empty of clouds and 'planes.
Where do you orbit, Johnny, overhead?
Red Squadron pancaked long ago at base.
O valiant young runner of no race,
Where do you fly? In what formation led
Do you keep station? Say, now, did clouds flash black
With winged destruction in swift curved pursuit
And life-entangled turn to negative,
Grey metal petals falling?

                O, did you wake
Big as forever in the split snap-second
That lies between the firing and the break?

ADVENTURE

W. Kynaston (Leading Air Woman)

Why must adventure stories be
Tales of the wild and restless sea?
For me the true adventure lies
Not in the sea but in the skies –
The wind outstripped, unfathomed space,
The changing moods of Heaven's face,
The thrill of speed, the sense of pow'r –
A lifetime in a crowded hour.

Look up, look up and see me soar
Up thro' the blue to Heaven's door!
My spirit's free, my heart is light:
I climb, I dive, I wheel in flight.
My God is here, I feel Him nigh!
Was ever man who lived as I?
Go take your wild and restless brine:
Mysterious space, unsearched, is mine!

A PSALM

Anonymous

My daughter,
Consider the ways of the WAAF,
Consider her ways, and be warned.

For behold, it hath come to pass
That she is no longer a WAAF
But a WD.
For she is to her Lord and Master
Neither an aid nor an auxiliary,
But an accomplice.
She trotteth in front of him on parade,
And bringeth his pace down to twenty-seven.
She strideth out, even as he does,
And forsweareth her glamour glide.
She swingeth her arms from the shoulder,
Gainsaying the precepts of her upbringing,
Whereby she was taught that all movements
Of a lady shall be restrained.

She casteth aside her silly civilian hats,
And she clampeth on her brow a service hat
That is even sillier, and becometh her not.
She layeth away her dainty garments
And girdeth herself for battle,
Even in vestments like unto a coat of male,
A tunic and skirt
Designed by the Iron Duke himself.
She may carry neither bag, fur, nor umbrella,
Yea, rather, she must conceal her compact,
Lipstick, hankie, and her what-nots
In the tunic pockets provided for this purpose.
She forsweareth the silken snare of hose,
And bindeth her nether limbs in stockings
Of grey canvas.
How beautiful are feet in shoes,
Yea, in shoes of fine leather, gondola-built.

She disdaineth her garments with much derision,
And laugheth them to scorn.
Yet I say unto you,
She would not exchange them for a queen's raiment.
Sweeter to her are they than a sequined jacket,
A coat of many chinchillas.
Dearer are they than ninety cents a day.
She crieth aloud over her toil and tribulation
As she polishes the badge and buttons of the RCAF.
Yet neither heaven nor hell nor principalities
Nor powers could separate her from them.
She shineth in the noonday hour and knoweth,
In her secret heart, that Solomon was not arrayed
Like one of these WD.

For her troubles she must suffer
Calumny from civilians,
Orders from officers,
And whistles from airmen.
She may not mix with officers,
Nor may an airman
With his strong right arm
Carry her,
Lest she dash her foot against a stone.
She may not loiter in the paths of dalliance
Entering into her barracks at night.

Yea, my daughter, consider the ways of the WD.
But she would not change her lot.
And if you, too, in the stubbornness of your heart,
Thou, too, must join the WD . . .
Then go, thou wayward one!
Thy ways may not lead to pleasant places –
But Lucifer himself shall not be a patch
To thy pride.

CARRY ON!

(A Leading Air Woman's Lament)

This familiar expression leaves one the impression
   The phrase has been left incomplete.
"Carry on!" Carry what? Or at least – carry where?
   We seem to be dangling in air!
To reach a solution and end this confusion
   I've checked all available sources,
In hopes that some history might solve the mystery –
   "From whence came this phrase to our Forces?"
I've been reading text books (found in library nooks)
   I've searched and researched – but in vain!
Who first "coined" this phrase? Was it general or sage?
   Or some genius of whimsical brain?
I have read KR (Air), but there's no reference there,
   And that "bible" of air force procedure –
Known as AF-RO's – has no clue to disclose . . .
   Now I'm reaching the end of my lead, Sir!
"Carrying on" (where I come from) refers to uncouth fun –
   An alliance, in truth, quite illicit.
"Carrying on" is, in fact, Sir, a treacherous act, Sir!
   Now, how can I be more explicit?
I should like to point out (should there be any doubt)
   Though I joined this air force to give service,
It was never my aim to defame my good name –
   Understandably, Sir, I'm quite nervous!
My good reputation has been my salvation,
   So please, Sir, I prithee – in song –
When we meet on that route and I turn to salute . . .
   Restrain that refrain – "Carry On!"

Cupid Has Wings, Too

So many crazy and weird situations arose during the war to thwart Cupid's affairs. It was terribly difficult to conduct a romance with any continuity or endurance when instant transfers and postings could suddenly put oceans between you and your intended. With so many unexpected variables liable to intrude at any time, even the most informal wedding was in jeopardy. Many of the girls in Newfoundland resorted to proxy weddings as the only way around the situation.

I attended one during a Christmas leave in Cornerbrook in 1944. The bride was a Newfoundland airwoman stationed at Gander, and the groom was an American sailor who was somewhere on the high seas. One of the groom's pals served as groom and it was a really confused affair. Their wedding had been postponed so many times that they were determined to get on with the rites no matter what!

The following spring the bride was able to get leave and go south to Boston. There, the happy couple had their marriage blessed by the groom's pastor.

*　　*　　*

I had a date to meet my boyfriend at the local jewellery store to pick out my wedding band. When I arrived at the store I found his best pal waiting for me. He explained that the air force had decided that my boyfriend was required elsewhere at that moment.

When we walked into the store the clerk gave us the strangest look. He couldn't take his eyes off my companion. When he discovered what I wanted he really got agitated, and I wondered what was wrong.

It turned out that my companion had taken his own girl to the same store for her wedding ring just a few days earlier. When this was explained to the puzzled clerk things settled down and we all had a laugh.

*　　*　　*

We had an airman at No. 3 Service Flying Training School, Calgary, during the war who got his WD girlfriend "in trouble." In those wartime days one rarely heard the word "pregnant." The most common phrase used, at least in polite society, was: "She's

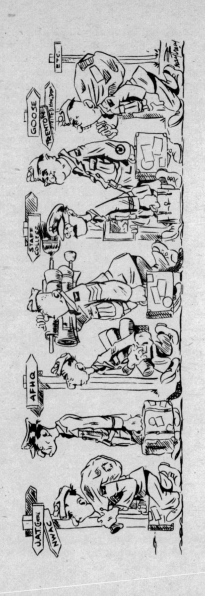

that way" – although "She's expecting," was okay, as was "She's in the family way."

For married girls, of course, it was a little easier to talk about pregnancy – but the action word for unmarried girls was panic. The stigma of having a child "out of wedlock," and the trauma of facing family and friends was truly overpowering. Not to mention the problem of the official wrath of the RCAF.

In this case, it was no less traumatic for the airman in question, and he sought advice from each of us in the hangar where he worked. A couple of airmen were all too eager to offer up remedies that might solve the fellow's problem.

One Corporal, with complete assurance, told him that it was a piece of cake. "Look, here's all you have to do. Take your girl and book a room at the Paliser Hotel downtown for the weekend. Buy yourself a bag of onions, borrow a hotplate and a big pot, and you're all set."

"What do you mean?" asked the frantic airman. "What am I supposed to do with onions and a hotplate? What good will they do?"

"Calm down, for Christ's sake!" the Corporal told him. "Don't you know nothing? You peel the onions and boil them up. Then you peel down your girlfriend and sit her on the boiling onions for the weekend. Bingo!"

The airman followed the instructions to the letter, and his girlfriend sat over the boiling onions all weekend. On Monday they went off and got married.

*   *   *

When Doug and I were planning to marry in April 1945, I went to the Medical Officer on the station to get some advice on birth control. The woman doctor was very easy to talk to. She measured me for a diaphram and advised me on the proper care. After each usage I was to rinse it out in warm water using mild soap flakes. Then I was to dry it with a terry cloth towel, sprinkle it generously with baby powder, and store it away in its case.

"This reminds me of an experience I had at my last station," the officer told me. "An unwed airwoman reported on sick parade one morning, and we soon discovered that she was two months pregnant. The poor thing told me that she couldn't understand how she got that way. 'We took precautions every time,' she said. 'My boyfriend used a condom and he always washed it out afterwards with Rinso . . . .' Lord! Can you imagine how rotten that 'skin' must have been? I'll bet it was like a sieve – and I'll bet the airman's name was something like MacTavish! Do you realize that airmen are issued those things free of charge?"

I wasn't familiar with contraceptives at that time, so much of what she said went over my head. After Doug and I were married I told him the tale, and he had a great laugh.

* * *

Early in November 1944 the RCAF decided to reduce the airwoman strength of the service, and began by announcing that all married WD's were to be processed for discharge. We were told that there would be a meeting to discuss procedures the following morning.

It was more of a revelation than a meeting. Many of our girls had married secretly. American sailors and airmen were forbidden to marry until they returned to the United States – but you can't halt the course of true love, and marriages had flourished despite official orders.

When the married girls assembled our eyes bulged and our tongues wagged like crazy. Most of the marriages had been so secret they came as complete surprises.

The next day, a special issue of Daily Routine Orders carried several pages of "Change of Name on Marriage." And then the whole camp joined in the gossip.

* * *

We were married on a Saturday morning in the station chapel in the presence of half the people on camp. All of Bob's squadron was on hand, as well as my friends from barracks. They were doing their damndest to unnerve me.

The reception was held at the crew Mess and the Commanding Officer, who was my boss, gave the toast to the bride. My cheeks turned scarlet when he mentioned how I usually used every afternoon coffee-break for a visit to the hangar to see my beloved. I hadn't realized he was on to me.

146

Following the reception, Bob and I were to catch the ferry flight going out to Dorval. I had only to collect my bag from barracks. When the time came to leave I rushed into the barracks, grabbed my case, and dashed out.

Everything went smoothly, and we were soon in Montreal at our hotel. But when I went to open my bag there were no keys! I had fastened them to the handle of my suitcase and obviously the kids had removed them. I had to borrow the top from Bob's pyjamas to sleep in on my wedding night. Inside that damn suitcase lay all my dainty trousseau.

Next morning, Bob put through a call to base and arranged to have the keys flown out on the scheduled flight that day. I was so damn furious with those kids back at camp! But late in the afternoon we caught a cab to the airport to pick up the keys, and everything went well for the remainder of our leave. In fact, the absence of my civilian clothes worked a bit in our favour. I had to wear my uniform out to the airport – and when the cabbie learned that we were on our honeymoon he would only charge us for a one-way trip.

*   *   *

In 1942 I was stationed at Air Force Headquarters in Ottawa, where I worked in the Records Section as an Administration Officer. My husband, Ken, had also been posted in Ottawa, and he worked in the Casualties Section at Dow's Lake. Because of my married status, and because I was twenty-five and considered mature enough to conduct myself properly (what did the RCAF know?) I was granted permission to live out of barracks.

Housing was very scarce, so we were fortunate indeed when we located a furnished, two-bedroom flat in the Sandy Hill part of the city. We offered to share it with two former college pals from McGill University. Chuck had been posted from the station at Trenton, and was working as an Accounts Officer at another temporary building located on Elgin Street across from the Lord Elgin Hotel. His wife, Kitty, was a civilian who worked at the head office of the Bank of Canada. Although they had found accommodation in the Glebe district, they could not take possession for another month. We invited them to use our spare bedroom until that time.

The apartment was crowded – but since we didn't spend a great amount of time there it didn't matter. There was plenty to do in Ottawa despite the wartime atmosphere, and the four of us enjoyed many an evening relaxing in the Grill Room of the Château Laurier Hotel, or trekking across the river to the Standish Hall. Often we would brave the long queues at one of the four movie houses in downtown Ottawa to view the latest J. Arthur Rank or Hollywood flick. Of course, there was also fun to be had at the Mess.

My cooking skills were limited at this time. I had only been married six months and my culinary specialties consisted of spaghetti and meatballs or roast beef and Yorkshire pudding. I was, however, a great little cake baker.

Kit's activity at the stove brought a bit of variety to our home-cooked meals. She was a firm believer in casserole dishes which could be prepared beforehand and dumped in the oven when we returned from work. These delectables – salmon loaf, meatloaf, and chicken or beef pie – were later added to my recipe file.

Due to the proximity of our sleeping quarters, life became fairly informal. It was impossible to keep those damn bedsprings from squeaking and squawking in the dead of night, and our conversations around the breakfast table were often uproarious – especially on Sunday mornings. Still, we managed to observe the proprieties.

At the end of our second week of communal living, Ken and I both managed to get a weekend break from duty. Kit was off to work on Saturday morning, and I thought that Chuck had also departed for Elgin Street when I staggered from bed. Ken and I would have the apartment to ourselves for the whole day!

Bleary-eyed, my hair in curlers, I stumbled down the short hallway to the bathroom. The door to the bathroom was ajar and, looking in, I could see my husband's naked back. He was clad in the brief kilt wrap-around I had given him for his birthday: a Cameron tartan print on terry-cloth lined cotton, which I thought would be useful in officers' barracks. He was standing on one leg, the other balanced on a bathroom stool, and he was leaning over to clip his toe nails.

The temptation was far too great for any red-blooded Canadian girl. I pushed the door gently open, slipped inside, reached my arm beneath his raised leg and upward under the wrap . . . . Finally, my fingers found what they were searching for and, giving it a tweak, I squealed, "Ding, Dong!"

The head above the partly-clad body turned – and Chuck gazed down on me with a wide grin. "Sorry, honey. Wrong number."

Uttering a scream I backed into the hall, where I collided with my husband just emerging from the kitchen with a startled expression on his mug. I could only stand there, blushing furiously and stammering, "He . . . he . . . he . . . he's got your kilt on!"

Ken's look of puzzlement changed immediately into a slow grin. "Sorry," he said to Chuck. "I really don't know what to do with this wench. There's no keeping her satisfied."

Chuck, grinning broadly from ear to ear, replied, "Yeah, but what a way to go! I'd heard these airwomen were a wanton breed. Maybe I should encourage Kitty to enlist."

For days, weeks, months, years, decades, I have been trying to live that incident down. But my three dearest people won't let me.

* * *

I fell in love in Victoriaville, Quebec, at Initial Training School. It was in 1943 and her name was Gertana. We met in the Café de Gaulle over a chocolate sundae.

It was winter in Quebec and bitterly cold, and there weren't many places an airman could romance his girl. We had no car and no money and Gertana's stepmother kept a careful eye on us when we sat in her tiny parlour. So we spent a lot of time in the Café de Gaulle, playing the juke box and listening to the Ink Spots singing "Paper Doll."

At ITS, the reward for successful achievement was the privilege of wearing battle-dress. I could hardly wait to show Gertana my new costume – except that it was strictly forbidden to wear battle-dress off the camp. When you are in love, however, anything is possible. I climbed the perimeter fence as soon as it was dark and set off to romance Gertana dressed like a real aircrew type.

The Service Police found us in our favourite booth at Café de Gaulle about thirty minutes later. Gertana spoke to them in French, and they agreed to allow me to escort her home before reporting to the guard house to be formally charged. I made the mistake of climbing back over the fence instead of going through the guard house as promised. Once in the barracks, my buddies insisted that I go back over the fence and through the guard house. While we debated, the Orderly Officer collected me and I was charged.

In the morning I was paraded before the Commanding Officer, who was a Squadron Leader. This guy resembled a Japanese Emperor. He never smiled, and we students all feared him. I remember only one thing the CO said to me (although his harangue was long and loud). He asked me if I had ever heard the story of the cat and the train. When I replied that I hadn't, he told it to me:

"A cat was walking over the railway tracks when a train came along and ran over its tail. The cat turned around quickly to see what had happened to its tail and the train cut its head off. The moral of the story – and my advice to you, young man – is simple. Don't lose your head over a piece of tail."

* * *

A short time after World War Two I found myself navigating a Canso (an amphibious flying boat) around the Canadian north country. After a particularly hard landing one day, we had to fly south to Calgary for repairs.

That evening, I took the opportunity to head into town to find some female companionship – something that had been sadly lacking up north. After I had "corralled" one of Calgary's beauties, we made our way to the Officers' Mess at Curry Barracks.

We soon developed a warm glow of mutual appreciation for one another at the bar, and decided that a visit to my Canso aircraft (now parked on the flight line) would be an excellent idea. Here I introduced my bosom friend to the rest-bed, an integral part of that aircraft. But I doubt that our use of the bed was the one the designer intended.

The following morning, as we took off and headed north, I was positioned in one of the "blisters." These were two large convex perspex bubbles, one on each side of the aircraft in the aft section. They lifted upward to provide entrance to the aircraft, and had been used as gun positions in wartime. I was sharing the compartment with an Ottawa bureaucrat whom we were transporting north on some government mission. As I sat there, enjoying the view, something caught my eye on the floor of the aircraft. I looked down to see something pink. When I picked it up I wasn't too surprised to discover that it was a pair of pink panties.

Not wanting the bureaucrat to see them and get the idea that the RCAF operated a flying brothel, I thought I'd better dump them overboard. Fast! But every time I opened the window my companion looked my way. My chance finally came as we passed over Edmonton – and I breathed a sigh of relief as I threw them out.

There have been times, in the quiet hours since then, when I have wondered what the good citizens of Edmonton thought as a pair of lacy, pink panties floated down over their fair city on a beautiful summer day.

* – * *

On our final weekend at Rockcliffe Manning Depot we were given thirty-six hour passes, and I was able to spend that weekend in Ottawa with my parents. It would be my final visit home for the next sixteen months.

Returning to camp on Sunday night, I was descending from the streetcar in front of Charles Ogilvy's store on Rideau Street when there was a sudden blur of official, air force blue. I sprang to attention and produced my very first salute. A magnificent salute if I do say so, myself. The officer stood there gazing down at me in amazement before, in rather desultory fashion, he returned my salute.

The bus for Rockcliffe arrived seconds later, and I jumped aboard and took a seat. Then – to my horror – I realized that the officer had followed me on board and was seating himself beside me.

We had been taught, during our four-week course, that we did not consort with male officers on or off the station. We had also been told that we saluted the uniform – not the person wearing the uniform. I was beginning to fear that the gentleman inside this official suit of blues had misinterpreted my intentions. I noticed that he was only a mere Pilot Officer, and was much younger than he had appeared to be outside in the twilight.

"Do you have to salute officers?" he asked.

I explained the facts of WD life to him, with particular emphasis on our instructions not to speak to or consort with male officers. He received all this with an expression of incredulity.

As our bus continued its journey he told me he had just returned from service in India. He had received his commission while based overseas, and there had been little saluting. "Only when you happened to encounter a senior hardhat on your route," he explained.

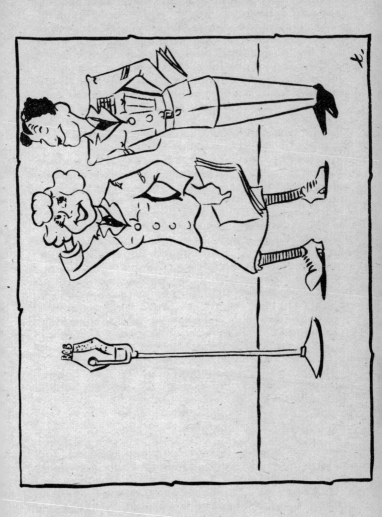

I told him that if he were to remain in Ottawa he would have to get accustomed to saluting.

At the next bus stop, Anne, a girl I knew from church activities entered the bus. She looked at me in amazement, spoke rather stiffly, and plopped herself down on the seat directly in front of me. Obviously, she took a dim view of seeing me in uniform.

I was becoming more agitated by the minute because my companion was bringing the conversation around to the inevitable – trying to wangle a date. I knew that Anne must realize I did not know the officer seated next to me, and was thinking "pick up." I explained to the officer that I would only be at Rockcliffe a few more days, and would have no time for dating.

The conversation then turned to India, and by the time Anne exited the bus on the Montreal Road I was being given an interesting description of Indian women: their dress and life-style. A subject matter above all possible criticism.

I fully expected the young officer to continue on his way down the road to the lower station when we debarked from the bus at Rockcliffe. But to my consternation he continued towards our WD camp, explaining that the quarters for repatriated officers were located directly across the road from our WD barracks.

I was beginning to quake in my new issue shoes. What if I should encounter an officer or even a non-commissioned officer? I thought I would really be in trouble. Well, I didn't meet an officer – but when we neared the WD lounge we ran into a group of girls from my squad who followed us to the barracks area. When I entered the building they swarmed all over me, giving me a bad time about picking up young Pilot Officers!

It took the remainder of my stay at Rockcliffe to live this down – but I never forgot my first encounter with the male world of RCAF officialdom.

*　*　*

I was one of a number of airwomen chosen to attend a party honouring a group of Russian naval officers who were visiting port. It turned out to be a crazy night!

The Russians couldn't speak any English – at least most of them couldn't – and we had to converse through translators and hand signals. The chap who was my escort could speak a little English, but only very haltingly. His name was Valerie, which I had always thought was a woman's name. It was just one of the things I learned that evening.

They were most pleasant gentlemen – and great dancers as well. Before the evening was over the WREN's and WD's were dancing with the Russians, doing a Russian version of the polka to American pop tunes of the day. We danced to "Down by the Ohio," "Pennsylvania Polka," "Roll Out the Barrel," and many others.

One of the airwomen even received a proposal of marriage. A Russian asked her: "Would you please marry up with me?" She declined.

* * *

I was on leave in London and walking through Hyde Park one day with a fellow WD from Montreal. We were knitting as we walked, strolling along, our needles keeping time to our chatter, when unexpectedly we heard the sound of pounding feet behind us. Someone called out, "Hey, girls, hold up! You've dropped something."

We stopped and turned around to find a young Pilot Officer, red-headed and freckle-faced, running up to us with a ball of blue wool in his hand. He was busy winding the wool as he ran. "You dropped your wool away back there!" He gestured behind him. "I've been trying to catch you."

Five months later I married that redhead, and ever since he has continued to rewind my wool for me.

* * *

The WD's and WREN's on duty in wartime Newfoundland could afford to be very choosy when it came to dating because there were so many men to every girl. Romances flourished, and over forty girls in our group were married in relatively short order. One marriage was quite romantic.

Hazel Wilson, an airwoman Sergeant, was along with us on the day a group of airwomen and Yanks took a dory out for a close look at an iceberg that was lodged in Quidi Vidi gap. When one of the Yanks became too inquisitive and fell overboard into the murky, ice-cold water, Hazel jumped in and hauled him to safety.

Later, she was awarded a Life Saving Medal amid a lot of pomp and circumstance.

That life she saved became her husband after the war.

* * *

We had great dances in the airwomen's lounge at Gander, Newfoundland. There were never enough women to go around, and I remember one time when an airman turned up with his own "date." He had borrowed a mop from the kitchen and attached a cross-beam below the mop-head, for arms. Then he had dressed his scarecrow in an old issue uniform he had borrowed from one of the airwomen, perching one of the old, squat hats on top of it all.

He introduced his partner as Corporal Broom, and told us: "She hangs out in the kitchen."

Stranger Than Fiction

A few months after my eighteenth birthday I decided that I should "do my bit" for King and Country. But which service should I join? Being only five feet, zero inches tall, the thought of dragging a heavy rifle around in the army didn't sound like fun. And being at sea for months on end with the navy didn't appeal to me, either. Since I was living in Winnipeg, the heart of the Commonwealth Air Training Plan, I wanted to fly. So it was relatively easy to decide on the RCAF. (I had also heard that the air force slept between white sheets.)

On my first visit to the Recruiting Unit I was told to "go back to high school." I looked younger than my age – but I finally got over that hurdle by showing the Recruiting Officer that I had *graduated* from high school.

The next problem was the physical exam. After some preliminary questions the Medical Officer told me that I was not only too short but too skinny, as well. He said there was no point in going any further with the medical exam. After going back several times I finally got the MO to agree that if I could bring my weight up to 100 pounds, he would give me the rest of the exam.

After some weeks of stuffing myself with chocolate bars, gallons of malted milkshakes, and assorted pies and cakes (in between meals), I returned to the Recruiting Unit, drank a quart of water, and tipped the scales at 100 pounds. I had only weighed ninety pounds the first time.

The MO kept his word, and found that – aside from my height and weight – I was physically fit. He said, however, that there was still one problem. The official height and weight minimums for the RCAF were five feet, three inches and 115 pounds. Luckily for me, the doctor was a very practical person. He rationalized: "I can't expect you to weigh 115 pounds when you're only five feet tall, and I can't expect you to be five feet, three inches when you only weigh 100 pounds. So you pass."

Although getting accepted into the RCAF was a major difficulty, it certainly wasn't the end of the problems I had with my height. Or lack of it. The trip through clothing stores to get outfitted was the next disaster.

Not only were the jackets and pants too long, but my boots would still be pointing straight ahead after I had done an about turn. The most unusual problem was with the rubber raincoat the supply clerk handed over. The arms came down to my ankles while

the bottom of the raincoat got caught under my boots. The supply clerk rectified this by producing a large pair of shears. He shortened my sleeves – which was okay – but when he shortened the coat he almost cut off the pockets. I was lucky that you weren't allowed to go around with your hands in your pockets or I would have looked like the hunchback of Notre Dame.

Next came parades at good old Brandon Manning Pool. "Sizing" was no problem for me. On the order: "Tallest on the right, shortest on the left, in three ranks, size!" I simply made a left turn, marched a few yards, and then let the flight form up on me. Then (after some mysterious manoeuvre) I would end up in the middle of a rank. Sometimes, before sizing, I would have a tall chap on either side of me – and when we spaced, the fellow on my left would put his fist on the shoulder of the fellow on my right. I would be standing under his arm. The drill Corporal never appreciated our sense of humour. When the rest of the flight was marching with a "standard" pace I was almost splitting myself in half trying to stretch my legs to keep in step. It was either that or take twice as many steps as everyone else.

Even the ordinary morning ablutions weren't a simple task. Everyone had a tin washbasin – except I needed two. One to stand on and the other to use. Otherwise, I couldn't see in the mirror. Even the height of the urinals posed a problem.

Despite everything I managed to survive Manning Pool and was posted to Initial Training School at Regina. Here, if I passed the ground school, I would be chosen for either pilot or navigator training. Well, I was probably the only guy to go through ITS without training on the Link Trainer. This was because of my "cockpit check" in the Tiger Moth. I couldn't reach the rudder bars with my feet.

It was at ITS that I received my nickname, "Sea Level." One day we were learning about the altimeter and the fact that its calibration is based on a sea level standard pressure of 29.92 inches of mercury. This was as low as you could go . . . . I've been stuck with that name to this day. Once a letter was actually delivered to me when the only address was: *"29.92" RCAF Station Greenwood, Nova Scotia.*

The last step towards getting my navigator's Wings was the ground training and flying training at No. 7 Air Observers School, Portage La Prairie, Manitoba. Unlike the rest of the trainee navigators, I made two uses of my sextant box. I used it to carry the sextant to the aircraft; and then I used it to stand on, so that I could see through the astrodome of the Anson to take a star shot.

Finally, the big adventure! I graduated and was shipped overseas to England. Here the RAF attempted to issue me with a battle-dress uniform. Well, the only uniform that they had small enough for me was a WAAF's uniform. This was fine as far as the shoulders, arm-length, and waist were concerned – but I needed two pillows to fill out the chest. It was fortunate for me that I eventually received my commission, and was then able to purchase a tailor-made officer's uniform.

We sat around England waiting for an opening at an Advanced Flying Unit, and to fill the void I was posted to an RAF regiment station for escape and evasion training. My height had some advantages – and some disadvantages – in these escape and evasion exercises. I found it fairly easy to hide myself, and getting under barbed wire fences and crawling through pipes was a snap. Scaling an eight-foot wall was a bear, however. And I still remember one small creek we had to cross. Everyone else sailed across it but when my turn came I landed right in the middle, wet and mad.

Eventually, I passed through the Advanced Flying Unit and Operational Training Unit and was posted to 434 Squadron at Croft, Yorkshire. We had Halifax bombers. Now, you get into a Halifax by going up through a trap door in the floor of the fuselage. Standard procedure in our crew was for me to toss my parachute and other equipment up through the hole; then one of our crew would toss me up after it.

On our twenty-fifth trip our crew was forced to bail out over England. I was the first one out the hatch – and yet our mid-upper gunner claimed that he landed and had three pints of beer at a local pub before I hit the deck!

*   *   *

We had a guy working in the Accounts Section who was famous for not washing his socks. He would wear them until they were stiff, and then throw them out and scrounge another pair.

Once, we had a Public Relations Officer posted in who was an amateur hypnotist. He gave a demonstration in the Sergeants' Mess, picking our dirty-sock friend as his subject. He told him that when he awoke he would go immediately to his barracks, wash out all his socks and underwear, and plan to be on hand next morning bright and early for church parade.

With a snap of the fingers our subject was awakened. He looked around at us with a puzzled expression for a moment, then he leaped to his feet and went straight to his barracks. In the morning, when we arrived for parade, there he was: all bright and shining.

Unfortunately, the hypnotic trance didn't last. The following Sunday our friend just made it to parade – and he was sockless. He got a real case of blistered heels.

*   *   *

We had returned to barracks late one night after working the night shift in the Filter Room. Ruth and I were in the laundry area, washing out some clothing, when another WD suddenly entered the room.

At first we thought she was a couple of sheets to the wind. Then we realized that she was sleep-walking. She had a very dazed expression on her face, and she muttered to us about "looking for it." Ruth asked her what she was looking for, but she only mumbled something incoherent and headed out of the room. Curious, we were following her, when she abruptly stopped in her tracks and declared, in a really loud voice: "I've simply got to find it. I can't balance the pay records until I find it!" Then she headed back to the laundry room and, once more, we followed along.

All at once another girl appeared and took her by the arm. "Come on, Bea," she said. "It's awfully late, and you've got to get some sleep." Then she led her away. But in a few minutes the companion returned to tell us that Bea worked in the Accounts Section. "She's always talking in her sleep – adding up totals. Sometimes we can ask her what she's doing and she answers us – we have a lot of fun with her – but this is the first time she's walked in her sleep. I guess she can't balance her books again. Wait till I tell her about this adventure tomorrow morning!"

*   *   *

When the air force began flying jet fighters after the war, no one had given a thought to noise levels or to protective devices for the

groundcrews. But Air Defence Group at St. Hubert, Quebec, quickly became concerned when hearing problems were reported among flight-line crews. What to do?

Ear plugs were found to be impractical. Earphones seemed a better idea, but the radio-type headset then in use didn't block the damaging high frequencies. The Senior Engineering Officer and the Senior Medical Officer who were wrestling with the problem decided that some type of foam lining, inserted into the earphones, might be an answer. A muff of some type. But what?

Feeling stymied by the problem, the Engineering Officer decided to take a shopping trip to Montreal. Perhaps window shopping would suggest a product or an idea that would lead to a solution. He found the answer staring at him from the window of a ladies' dress shop. The smallest pair of falsies on the market.

With some embarrassment he purchased a set and hurried back to base. When fitted into specially formed ear-pieces they served admirably as prototype ear protectors.

Could any airman ask for more?

* * *

I was stationed at Grand Forks, North Dakota, with a NORAD unit. This was in the early sixties. We were only about 100 miles directly south of Winnipeg, which was easily reached if we wished to spend a weekend in Canada.

I had several United States Air Force airmen working for me, and they were guaranteed to provide some interesting happenings at least once a week. One Monday morning, a huge black airman who answered to the name of Willy stepped into my office and asked if he could show me something. I told him to go ahead.

"Suh," the airman said, "this here's a citation from the Winnipeg police. Now, ain't that real pretty, suh?"

He handed over a handsome-looking plaque bearing the coat of arms of the City of Winnipeg. There was an inscription on it, praising the airman for services to the city.

Dumbfounded, I asked, "What did you do to get this, Willy?"

"Well, suh," related Willy, "I goes up to that Winnipeg on the weekends. To get me some of that little white leg, you know? A time or two ago I got to thinking, man, you know, I should report these here girls to the authorities. Don't seem right they chargin' me all that money.

"Well, suh, the police, they was mighty pleased to hear about them girls. Yes, suh. They say to me, Willy, ever' time you has one of them gals, you reports to us.

"Now, suh, I been doin' this regular. 'Course that way I don't have to pay none, neither. But they sure was mighty pleased, suh, and that why they give me this citation."

*   *   *

It became the custom, after I joined the Mess, for the other WD's to sit around until I had finished my dinner so that I could read their teacups. It was a bit of fun I had picked up from my mother, who always ran the tea shop at the church bazaars and read the ladies' cups.

On an evening in late October we were at our usual places, but I had begged off, saying I was too tired. One of the girls, Irene, pleaded with me to make an exception in her case, since I hadn't read her cup for more than a week. After much pleading I reluctantly took her cup – and was immediately horrified at what I saw. Trying to put her off, I placed her cup down and said that I really was too tired. But she insisted.

At a complete loss on how to proceed I finally asked, "Irene, do you have someone close to you in the air force?" She said that she didn't think so. "Are you sure?" I queried. "A cousin or close friend, perhaps?" Irene replied that she didn't have anyone and wondered why I asked.

"Well, according to your cup," I told her, "you are going to hear of someone very close to you who will be killed in a plane crash . . . ."

Irene was a sunny, open-hearted girl, and everyone liked her. She had been in Newfoundland when I got there in 1943, and many a night, when I came off the late shift and she came in from a date, we would spend some time swapping lines of poetry. She revelled in it; and since we both had a good fund of it in our memories we used to have a wonderful hour or two reciting our favourite pieces.

And now this was in the tea leaves. A plane nose diving into the ground with Irene beside the plane. I was very upset, and tried my best to put it out of my mind.

There was an RCAF coastal patrol base at nearby Botwood, and any time they had a dance they would fly a Canso over to pick us up since there were no WD officers at Botwood. A bunch of us flew over for the November Eleventh dance that year, and had a grand time. We all flew back to camp on Monday. Irene, who was the Recruiting Officer for our area, decided that she might as well return to Botwood with the Canso crew. She was due there on Tuesday morning.

The flight was delayed for more than an hour while they waited for the Padre who was also going to be a passenger. The weather began to close in, darkness was approaching, and the crew started to grow anxious. They did finally get away – but their landing on the water at Botwood had to be made in bad weather and in darkness. The aircraft crashed, and Irene and the Padre were killed.

When I turned up for dinner that evening I hadn't heard the tragic news – and I was met by a row of faces all turned towards me. After they told me about the crash someone said, "Well, I guess you read Irene's teacup right, didn't you?"

Then it all came back to me. I never read another teacup after that.

* * *

It was July of 1944 when I crewed up at Abingdon, and then moved to Stanton Harcourt for training. Here we met the mighty Whitley bomber. Our kite was "U" Uncle, a nose-down, tail-up Whitley, whose friendly name was "the flying coffin."

As the rear gunner, I got more flying time than the rest of the crew. When we took off the skipper locked the brakes, opened the throttles, and pushed the stick forward. This made the rear gunner airborne. On landing, the rear gunner was the last to land – the very last – and always with a mighty thump.

One sunny day, we were detailed for bombing practice, and were loaded with ten-pound smoke bombs. I climbed aboard and into the rear turret. Reaching back, I pulled the small doors shut behind me and, still reaching back, made sure they were latched and locked. Then I did my normal checks and we were soon airborne.

The first run over the bombing range allowed the bomb aimer to get his wind drift figured out, but I was expected to provide the drift angle on subsequent runs. I did this by following the falling bomb in my gun sight, while reading off the drift from a green-and-red scale. This gave port or starboard drift in degrees. I had to relay this information over the intercom after each run. Down below I could see the target: some very small circles inside some more very small circles.

Our first two runs were pretty good, with one bomb very close and one inside the rings. I leaned back in my seat as the pilot circled for another run and reflected on a recent Headquarters order that had given me some trouble.

We had been warned that everyone wearing loose, zipper-type flying boots must have them modified. We were instructed to draw two straps from stores of the kind used on Mess tins. These were to be taken to the station cobbler who would sew them on your flying boots at ankle height. Finding the time to get to the stores – and then to the cobbler's – had been a real bind. But I had dutifully carried out orders. The object of all this was to prevent the boots from falling off if you bailed out.

On our number three bomb run I picked up the flight of the bomb through the gun sight, moving the guns and turning the turret at the same time. I had to lift from my seat to keep the gun sight tracking the bomb. The more I depressed the guns the more I lifted from my seat.

Finally, the bomb hit the target and I sat down and leaned back, glancing down to read the drift reading. Suddenly, I found myself leaning on air! As I felt myself falling out I must have hit the turret controls, for the turret swung completely abeam at the same time as my intercom came unplugged.

I don't remember my life flashing before my eyes. All I remember is a sudden jerk and complete terror. My fall had been stopped by a jolt which nearly broke my ankle. The newly-acquired boot strap had caught on the gun control – and I was left dangling by the most recent order of High Command! My parachute pack was safely stowed back in the fuselage while I lashed back and forth in the slipstream.

Meanwhile, the bomb aimer had not received any response from his request for the last drift angle, and he sent the second gunner back to investigate. All Reggie found in the turret was a boot and part of a leg.

It took a lot longer to get back in the turret than it did to get out. I couldn't climb up against the slipstream. The skipper tried putting his wheels and flaps down to slow the aircraft, but I *still* couldn't get back in. Finally – by bringing the aircraft almost to the stalling point – he reduced the speed enough so that I could crawl up my own leg. Back into that beautiful turret!

* * *

One of the most onerous duties an airman could be inflicted with was service in the funeral party of a fellow airman whose body had been shipped home for burial. The warning was always short and the practice time woefully inadequate. It took a bit of rehearsal to get the slow march under control; and if you were one of the firing party it was a bigger chore to get the rifles to fire all together.

When the whole affair was over there was always a great sense of relief. On the way home from the cemetery it was imperative to divert the transport so that the funeral party could relax over a pint or two. After all, the deceased would have wanted it that way.

On one such occasion, the funeral party had been hastily assembled at RCAF Station Sea Island, given the usual inadequate training, and driven into Vancouver to perform its solemn duty. To their surprise, everything that day went much as planned, and they were soon loaded onto trucks at the cemetery gates for the long ride back to Sea Island. Some of the firing party were marshalled into a panel truck without, as luck would have it, any NCO supervisor aboard. It was the perfect invitation to make use of an afternoon in convivial fashion.

One pub led to another as the afternoon wore on – and the once solemn firing party soon had their *joie de vivre* restored to them. It was a noisy and boisterous crowd of airmen who, after many false starts, finally climbed into the panel truck for the long ride home.

On the way through town the truck stopped at an intersection clogged with traffic. An airman decided that this was the perfect time to escape for another beer – and he jumped out the back door of the truck. Several others then decided to capture him – and they, too, jumped out and began chasing around in the stalled traffic. Since the fugitive was not very serious about escaping he was a perfect foil for his pursuers. Two chased him while a third, kneeling in marksman fashion, levelled his .303 rifle and fired a blank cartridge, left over from the funeral.

Down went the airman in a heap between the lines of traffic.

The two pursuing airmen grabbed him under the arms and dragged him back to the truck. They threw him inside and roared away, laughing hilariously at the terror-stricken motorists who had witnessed a "murder."

This great prank called for a celebration, and the van rolled merrily on to find yet another tavern. It was early evening when everyone decided that they had had enough for one day, and the party finally headed home to Sea Island. Each, of course, was on his best behaviour by this time, wearing the solemn face befitting a pallbearer.

They arrived at the camp gates and found, to their amazement, that a line of cars was being searched by police. Several police cars blocked the gates, and both civilian and military police were swarming around checking identifications.

It was only then, when there was no escape, that they learned how Vancouver radio stations had been blaring the news of an RCAF airman who had been slain in cold blood by his comrades. His lifeless body had been slung into a truck and driven off before the horrified eyes of hundreds of witnesses.

Jokers Wild

Practical jokes have always had a place in air force life, no matter how stringent the rules. It is doubtful that any raw recruit ever survived initial training without being sent down the hangar line for a pail of propwash. Today, props being scarcer, it is jetwash the sprogs are sent for. On the double.

At Trenton, circa 1949, a raw-boned lad showed up at the guard house, steeped in military lore learned from countless war movies. He was dressed in jeans and a cowboy shirt, cowboy boots, and a large, black Stetson. He had the manner of a cow puncher who could roll a cigarette with one hand – and he was a heaven-sent dream for every air force prankster. He bristled only slightly in the Mess when hoots and cowboy yells followed his every trip to the steam tables.

While awaiting assignment to a course the cowboy was put to work on the hangar line as GD: General Duties. This made him the chief entertainer for every groundcrew doing overhauls and aircraft checks. There were seven or eight hangars in a long line at Trenton in those days, and the walk from No. 1 to No. 8 was the better part of a mile.

On his first day, working at No. 1 hangar, the cowboy was sent on the long trek to No. 8 hangar to get two pails of prop pitch. When he arrived at No. 8 and explained his mission to a Flight Sergeant, he was presented with two buckets of lead shot, normally used to hold parachutes in place during repacking. The weight was enough to buckle the cowboy's knees – but he staggered away with the pails and finally arrived back at No. 1 hangar. Here, the NCO looked over the lead shot and declared that it was coarse pitch. He wanted fine pitch. And so back went the cowboy with the heavy buckets to No. 8 hangar. Various excuses and reasons kept him carrying the pails the entire day. He wasn't unduly perturbed since he had no suspicion that he was being had.

When the cowboy wasn't on a fool's errand, he was eagerly pursuing his main interest: looking for his first airplane ride. He made a request for a flight to everyone he met. It didn't take long before he asked the wrong person.

"Have you had your jump test?" asked the NCO. "You can't go up unless you understand about parachutes and how to jump properly."

An engine stand was quickly rolled across the apron to a grassy area. The cowboy was instructed to climb up to the top and then to

175

jump down, a distance of about ten feet. Time and time again he hit the dry sod with a thud and a groan – only to be told that he had failed to keep his feet together, or that he hadn't bent his knees correctly.

But persistence paid off, and before the afternoon was over he was graduated from his jump course with honours. The considerable audience cheered at his accomplishment as the cowboy, limping slightly, smiled proudly. Now he could get a ride in a Harvard aircraft.

If his fellow airmen had been cruel to him, the pilot who volunteered to take him aloft was little better than malignant. Off went the Harvard with its characteristic roar, and the cowboy had his first aerial view of the earth. But it was a short look.

Once clear of the runway, the Harvard went into a series of bone-crushing rolls, loops, snap rolls, and hammerhead stalls. All performed over the cheering crowd below. As the aircraft finally taxied in they saw a small, green face looking out of the rear cockpit . . . .

Eager offers of assistance were quickly followed by general consternation at the sight of the cowboy and the cockpit. Everything was wearing the cowboy's last three meals. He was much too sick to walk, let alone clean up the mess.

Unwittingly, the cowboy had turned the tables. The pranksters had to mop out the Harvard.

*　　*　　*

When I joined the RCAF in 1949, a seventeen-year-old kid from Nova Scotia, I was greener than grass. Everyone seemed so much more experienced and professional, especially the older guys.

Anyone wearing war ribbons could tell me anything – and I believed every word. One guy used to enthral me with his feats of derring-do in the skies over Europe. His Spitfire was always in the heat of action and full of bullet holes, and his hair-raising escapes from death kept my head spinning for weeks. Until I learned he was a cook.

At Camp Borden, where I was taking a supply technician course, the old Vets down at the hangar line would suck me into a game of pitching pennies to a line. When I had lost all my money and I'd ask them to buy me a Coke – I'd get a blast.

"If you haven't any money," they'd chorus, "don't come around here bumming!"

*   *   *

In 1943 I was building (or at least trying to build) my first radio from spare parts I had scrounged from here and there. I kept my pet project on the test bench in the Wireless Section and tinkered with it every chance I got. It was a godawful mess of wires – but it was mine.

After some weeks, I finally decided to test it out. It was lunch hour and there was no one else around. I snapped it on and – lo and behold – it worked! I couldn't believe my ears.

As I was standing back admiring my handy-work, I detected a puff of smoke coming out of the back of the radio. I quickly turned the set off and began pulling it apart looking for the trouble. I couldn't find a thing wrong in its interior.

I turned it on again, and soon another puff of smoke floated out. This time I thought I smelled tobacco. Curious, I began dismantling the radio, and in amongst the mess of wires I found a piece of plastic spaghetti. I picked up the end of the tiny tube and found that it led from the set across the test bench and through the wall into the next room . . . . Where I found a bunch of radio techs all pissing themselves with laughter.

*   *   *

When I was stationed at Air Defence Command Headquarters, I had an officer "friend" who developed a trick that never failed to make me violently angry. I got angry because in all the times I suffered through his joke, I never learned how to avoid it or how to cope with the results.

My "friend" materialized in the Mess any time I was talking to a particular Air Commodore: a man with absolutely no sense of humour. It was only after being cornered at the bar by this Air Commodore that I suddenly realized what might happen – and my eyes would begin a rapid search of the Mess as I wondered if my "friend" was on hand. He never failed me. Unable to escape a long and boring diatribe, I could do nothing but await my fate.

Thrusting his face between us, and ignoring the Air Commodore, my "friend" would say: "Hey, this guy sounds okay. I thought you said he was a prick!"

Another of his annoying tricks was to flick cold liquid on the back of some senior officer's neck during a Mess party. He would manoeuvre behind his victim and, with his handkerchief at the ready, dip his fingers into his drink. With a quick flip, he would spray the icy liquid on the guy's neck and at the same time yell KA-CHOO! putting his hankie to his nose.

The officer always reacted in the same manner. First a slow reddening of the neck from the collar to the hair line; and then a slow turn to see who would be so ignorant as to sneeze on a person's neck. By this time my "friend" was busy chatting with his companions, successfully appearing oblivious of the rage he had caused.

* * *

I had an airman pal in the RCAF who was an incorrigible practical joker. We alternated work at the Sergeants' Mess bar to pick up extra money. It was there that Mac and I ran into an associate member of the Mess who was very active in the Progressive Conservative Party. We told him that we would sure love to join up and work for the cause. Since there was an election due we were signed up immediately.

We didn't let the fact that neither of us had ever voted in a federal election bother us one bit. (Of course, the PC's that year didn't have a hope, so it didn't really matter.)

We had a marvellous time. We got to attend all the parties with all the free booze we could handle. In addition, friend Mac was given free gas for his car, and we had the opportunity to meet some pretty females.

Another joke centred around the card game Mac and I played each Friday night in the Sergeants' Mess. We held it in a little alcove that happened to be right next to the can. One day we arranged that I would bring some peanut butter to the game. I had it wrapped in wax paper and stuffed in a pocket.

That evening, just before it was my turn to deal the cards, I excused myself and went into the washroom. I smeared the peanut butter under the fingernails of my right hand, flushed the toilet (which was audible to the players), and resumed my seat at the card table.

When I proceeded to deal the cards, the guy on my right nearly barfed. He jumped up and went to stand at the far end of the bar, saying that he needed a breather. A minute later I joined him and, while talking away, casually draped my right arm over his shoulders – making sure I got my right hand in front of his face.

I'm sure if you asked him today you couldn't convince him that it was peanut butter on my fingers.

Mac was a serious coin collector, and one day he told me that he was being bugged by a young airman who professed to know everything about numismatics. Mac suggested that we set the guy up – and gave me some fairly valuable coins from his collection. One morning, when we were sitting with the young airman over coffee, I hauled these coins out of my pocket and told Mac that I had found them in my grandmother's attic in Nova Scotia. I didn't know if they were valuable or not, I said.

Mac took the coins and began examining them carefully, while our young friend had the fidgets. He never took his eyes off the coins. Finally, Mac tossed them on the table, and said, "I'll give you two bucks for them."

"Gee," I said, "that's great! Hand over the two bucks."

The young airman never spoke a word – but you could tell he was beside himself. After we returned to work he followed me around for most of the day, explaining how I had been taken.

*　　*　　*

When I was a WD during the war, I consistently attracted every weirdo, lame duck, drunk, and practical joker in Canada. I've never been able to fathom why. Maybe it was the uniform, but I'm not sure.

If I went to a movie, more often than seemed reasonable there was suddenly a hand on my knee and working higher. In those days I was too shy and naive to bat someone in the mouth. The only solution was to find another seat. If I'd gone to the show with a guy, it was simply a matter of changing seats. If I'd gone with another girl, we first had to locate empty seats – and those wartime theatres were always packed. Even then, I remember once being followed across the theatre. We went back to barracks a little earlier than we intended on that particular night.

Some nights we would go to the Service Centre to see what was

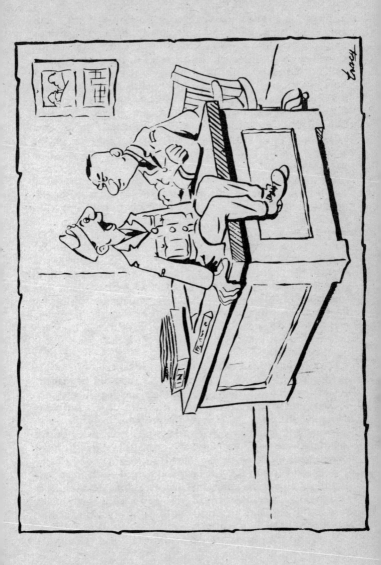

going on – and someone would always show up who was a little around the bend. While the other girls from our station jitter-bugged with sailors, we sat at lunch counters or in reading rooms, getting politely glassy-eyed as we listened to some guy going on and on, making no sense. The trouble was that we had been cautioned to beware of Repats. In time, I did figure out that Repats did not have horns and cloven hooves. They'd just been through a grinder that we could only faintly imagine, protected as we were. Still, some of the warnings lingered on, like echoes. One just never knew. So we were evasive but polite. The guy, in turn, finding what probably seemed a sympathetic ear, adopted us and clung like a burr.

Returning to barracks, especially by streetcar, was hazardous. The drunks came out of the woodwork. They would come staggering down the aisle, grabbing at the seatbacks to hold themselves up. Then, when they spotted you, they'd come to a dead stop, staring at the uniform (usually open-mouthed, so that you got the full blast of a day and night spent in the pub). They would sway there, hanging from a strap or leaning against your seat, while you dreaded the sudden lurch of the streetcar that would send them sprawling across the top of you. Of course they talked. Some were foul-mouthed. Most just over-friendly. If you answered it made things worse – and there was no escape because of the fine timing on which we operated. If we got off the car we'd be late through the guard house. We suffered so many of those endurance sessions on those trams.

Practical jokers were another matter. A host of them worked in our hangar. Everybody knows about the good old left-handed monkey wrench – but they had the girls looking all over for buckets of dihedral and prop wash. And then there was the day they wired the pencil sharpener to the generator.

My most infuriating encounter with a prankster came near the end of the war when everything and everyone was in transit. All of us were thinking about civilian jobs: *What do I do now?*

I was still bitten by the flying bug and wanted dearly to become an airline stewardess. Hearing that they were hiring stewardesses in Los Angeles, I arranged a final leave and headed south of the border. But the rumours turned out to be just rumours, and no one seemed to be hiring anybody.

I had arranged to stay at the Studio Club, and I found the

Hollywood Canteen a good place to have a snack while keeping my ears open to the latest rumours. Even with the war ending the place was swarming with uniforms. Everyone was drifting around, coming and going, comparing notes about what to do and where to settle. And everyone was delaying, reluctant to leave golden, warm California to cross the mountains into winter.

One day, as a group of us talked, a good-looking, blond, good-ole-boy type whisked out a pair of handcuffs and snapped them on my wrists. Everyone laughed. A real big joke. I laughed, too. But then he said he couldn't find the key and it suddenly wasn't funny for me.

The story became: I must have left it in my digs. With a pair of steel bracelets on my wrists I couldn't call the guy a liar, especially when he was a Sergeant as well as a Service Policeman.

Out on the street, all the passing shoppers and strollers paused or stopped to stare. A foreign uniform. What had she done? I couldn't very well yell at people that it wasn't what it seemed, that it was just a practical joke.

I thought about locksmiths. I thought about stores and hacksaws. Mostly I thought about losing good-ole-joe. But he wasn't figuring to get lost. Sticking like glue and grinning, he was still saying, "No, I don't have the key. Must have forgotten to put it in my pocket."

Meanwhile my temper was rising with each new problem. Like eating and drinking and using the bathroom.

Oh, yes, he found the key. With a beautiful gauging of my boil-over point!

*   *   *

Early in 1944 I was sent out to RCAF Station Torbay on temporary duty from No. 1 Group Headquarters. I was living at barracks with the airwomen based at Torbay, but was driven each morning to a remote site located several miles from the station. The operation was top secret at the time. The Canadian Army and the RCAF were conducting experiments on new materials to be used for Arctic clothing.

I was the only woman at this remote site, and on the first morning, the NCO in charge of the makeshift office where my desk and typewriter were located came to inform me that there was a woman's washroom positioned just inside the front entrance. I thanked him; but since I had no need to investigate at that moment, I went on with my work.

A little later in the morning, a second airman approached and gave me the same information. My curiosity was becoming whetted but I continued typing. At noon, when we broke for lunch, the NCO returned and suggested that I might want to use the washroom. Now I was thoroughly overcome with curiosity. "What is this, anyway?" I asked. "What's so fascinating about this women's washroom?"

"Well, you know," said the NCO, "we had to fix it up especially for you, and we just want to be certain that everything is okay."

I headed for the door marked "WD" – and immediately upon entering my eyes fell on a replica of one of those samplers pioneer women hung in their parlours. It read:

"Be it ever so humble there's no place like home!"

*   *   *

I had a really close airman friend in the RCAF who would get so hammered at night that he never remembered a thing the next day. One morning, for something to do, I told him: "Oh, brother, did you ever do it last night! You, friend, are in the deep stuff."

Alarmed, he asked me what he had done.

"Nothing spectacular," I shrugged. "You just tried to put your tool in Rita's hand when we were coming home on the bus."

"Oh, my God!" he cried. "You're putting me on."

"Nope," I said. "You do remember going to the fair in that little French village, don't you? Well, Rita was sitting with some WD's in the back of the bus and you kept taking your tool out and trying to put it in her hand."

"Ah, you're crazy," he snorted. "Hell, I'd never do anything that stupid!"

I let the matter drop and left him – but later in the day I saw Rita and told her what I had been up to. She was a good sport and agreed to go along with the gag.

That afternoon she managed to "accidentally" bump into my pal, and she suggested that he owed her an apology. That really did it. The poor bastard was scared stiff that his wife back in Canada would hear about his behaviour.

As reinforcement, and to make him a true believer, I lined up a few friends in the Corporals' Club that evening. On various occasions, well within earshot, they kept asking: "Who was that idiot on the bus last night with his tool out?"

That was the clincher. It was many weeks before the victim took another drink.

*   *   *

While attached to an auxiliary squadron after the war, I was gainfully employed in the retail trade. One day, I came upon a discarded mannequin. Taking it to the Mess, I hid it in the basement – and during a Mess party, I dressed it in my wife's old clothing, sneaked it into the men's washroom, and seated it on the toilet. As I left I pulled the door almost closed. Then I found a seat in the lounge where I could keep the washroom in view.

In a very short time a member of the Mess entered the washroom . . . and exited on the double with a shocked, open-mouthed look on his face. He went immediately in search of his wife so that she could tell the occupant of her error.

This gave me time to remove the mannequin and hide it once more in the basement.

When the wife appeared she marched rather dogmatically into the washroom. There she confronted a man in a most vulnerable standing position. Flying out of the bathroom, she went straight to her husband and accused him of playing a trick on her. I wonder why his pleading explanations were not believed?

*   *   *

When I was in the service I found that even the most harmless of practical jokes usually held a surprise for the practitioners. The result was never exactly as planned, and often astonished everyone. As Robert Burns so aptly put it in his poem: "The best laid schemes o' mice and men . . . Gang aft a-gley."

One of our squadron crews in Newfoundland had gone fishing on their day off, and they had caught a good-sized string of trout. They took the fish to the Mess to have them cooked for dinner, but they had caught so many that there was one large trout left over. During the discussion of what to do with it someone had the brilliant idea of stuffing it in Ralph's bunk. Ralph was a big, good-natured guy from Saskatchewan who never got ruffled about anything. He was also a guy who really liked his booze.

The fishermen took their catch to the barracks and gingerly placed it under Ralph's sheet and blankets. They fully expected that Ralph would find the fish when he went to bed and simply throw it out with a few, good-natured laughs – laughs in which everyone could join.

When Ralph did stumble home in the small hours he was feeling no pain. He undressed, slipped into his bunk, discovered the fish and, cradling it lovingly in his arms, went right off to sleep.

The rest of the crew couldn't believe their eyes, ears, or noses. The "joke" had fallen flat. There was the butt of their joke, arms around a large and very dead fish, sleeping like a baby. Disappointed with the lack of reaction the fishermen, too, fell off to sleep.

In the morning, the room was high with the stench of dead fish. Ralph was high, his bunk was high, and the whole barracks reeked. When Ralph awakened – he went from high to airborne. He flung the fish across the room and began cursing and raging and stomping around the barracks threatening, if he found him, to kill the son-of-a-bitch "who done that."

Across the Pond

I think I had more continuous fun in the RCAF during wartime than I had in the peacetime force. Perhaps that was due to the thought (always uppermost in my mind) that I might not live to a ripe old age – and so I went looking for extra excitement. But then, there were times in the postwar air force that matched or exceeded any wartime experience . . . .

When the Korean War broke out, I was lucky enough to be on exchange duties with the United States Air Force based in Hawaii. We flew transport aircraft on the Hawaii-to-Tokyo run – and it was in Tokyo that my American cousins introduced me to Japanese bath houses.

A lot of the guys referred to bath houses as "whore houses"; but I preferred to call them "cultural centres." I guess both terms were appropriate. There was no doubt that their prime purpose was to provide sex. In the more expensive ones, however, you were entertained by young ladies who had been trained to sing and play musical instruments. (My favourite instrument was a kind of Japanese banjo.)

The food they served in these bath houses was entirely memorable. It was eye-pleasing, delicious – and made even more palatable when served up at two in the morning after some six hours of soaking up rice wine.

Unlike Canadian whore houses, the bath houses did not have any girls living on the premises. Instead, there were 100 or so girls living close by in the neighbourhood who were on instant call. It was simply a matter of giving the "mama-san" or madame, a description of the girl you desired, and in a matter of minutes she was there. Most of the aircrew were easy to please. Their choice was usually a combination of beauty and breast size.

We used the Japanese measuring system where the best was Number One, tapering off to Number Ten – which stood for better than nothing. Ordering up a girl then became a relatively simple matter. Most of us went for girls with big knockers, called "chi chi" in Japanese. So we would ask the mama-san for "Number One chi chi, Number Ten face."

Before becoming sexually involved you were taken to the bathroom, where your girl would wash you down from head to foot with lots of soap and buckets of hot water. Then you entered a large, sunken bath filled with water almost at the boiling point. We all had various explanations for this. One firmly-held belief

was that the extremely hot water made you infertile. Another bit of folklore held that the boiling water killed any infectious diseases. I never did hear a Japanese reason. In any case, once the shock of entering that steaming water was overcome you were left with a feeling of relaxed contentment. It seemed so civilized in comparison to our North American customs.

Eventually, as the Korean War progressed and my trips to Tokyo became routine, I became a connoisseur of Japanese bath houses. When I heard one day that a new one had opened, I promptly paid it a visit. There I learned that the mama-san had lived in Vancouver for a number of years. She spoke English quite fluently. I spent several hours with her drinking saki, and we became very good friends.

Finding that I was a frequent visitor to Tokyo and that I stayed sometimes as long as two weeks, she suggested that I might like to go into business with her. The idea was for me to advertise her new bath house among the troops. She handed me a bunch of her calling cards and told me to sign my name on the back of each card before handing it to a fellow serviceman. For every six cards that turned up at her door, I would get one free night.

I figured: what the hell! why not? There weren't that many perks available in the RCAF in those days. I agreed to the scheme – but I often wondered what the official RCAF would say if they knew that they had an officer pimping for a Japanese whore house.

*   *   *

A Squadron Leader serving in India found a very good batman. He was not only reliable but, even more miraculous, he was honest. When the war ended, the Squadron Leader was ordered home to England for discharge. He decided to take his batman with him and make him his valet in civilian life.

Although the batman was willing to go, he said that he didn't know what he would do in an old English country home.

"Oh, I say, old chap," the Squadron Leader told him, "you do everything the same as you are doing here in India. It's all frightfully simple."

Then came the first morning in England, after the Squadron

Leader had arrived home to be reunited with his joyful wife. The couple were still sleeping when the batman entered the bedroom.

Placing a tray with tea for one on his master's bedtable he said, "Wakey, wakey, sir. Char's up." Then, walking around the bed, he threw back the covers exposing the nude wife. Slapping her smartly on the ass he yelled, "Come on, girl, wakey, wakey. Back to the village!"

* * *

When my husband and I were stationed at Metz with the Air Division we took our first furlough in September. It was a conducted tour of the Rhineland, Belgium, and Holland, and we went with my cousin Jack and his wife, who were stationed at Wiesbaden. The tour was to end in Paris, and I was eagerly looking forward to my first visit to that wonderful city.

When we reached Paris, our party of four had been expanded to eight by the addition of two American naval couples. We all decided that on this, our final night, we would abandon the official tour and dine at a posh supper club, renowned for its entertainment.

We were escorted into a very elegant room and seated at the end of the floor, adjacent to the performing area. Behind our table stretched a large, black curtain. It wasn't until we were well into our meal that we discovered what lay behind that curtain – and as the evening progressed, the scenario that unfolded behind it was more entertaining than anything happening on stage.

All eight of us were new to France and not well-versed in the customs of the French: which was why, I suppose, we all jumped when we heard a toilet flushing just behind the curtain. We soon became aware that the only thing separating us from the female entertainers' washroom was the flimsy curtain.

Clad in our finery, sitting amid all the grandeur and splendour of the supper club, our ears were assailed by the rude noises and loud conversations coming through the curtain. Our imaginations were flashing visions far more fascinating than anything on stage. It was a memorable meal! But we all laughed so much I can't recall what we ate.

* * *

Pilots who held desk jobs at Air Division Headquarters in Metz did their monthly proficiency flying at Grostenquin, one of the four RCAF fighter bases in Europe in the early 1950s. There they had mighty, twin-engined C-45 Expeditors or T-33 Silver Stars to wrestle around the sky.

One such "desk pilot" was a Wing Commander with an unshakable French-Canadian accent. He was well-known throughout the service not only for his accent and his war record, but for his sense of humour. This Wingco was airborne one day in an Expeditor, in contact with the Grostenquin Control Tower. With nothing much to break the monotony, the Tower operators decided to have some fun with the Wingco.

After some preliminary verbal skirmishes in which they pretended that they were having difficulty hearing his transmissions, and after asking him continually to repeat his requests, one of the controllers called: "Airforce 234 this is Grostenquin Tower. Could you r-o-u-n-d out your words a bit more. Please try to r-o-u-n-d your words. Over."

The Wingco was just as quick as his pranksters. He pressed his mike button and said: "Harse Hole. How's dat?"

* * *

When I look back at those great days spent with the RCAF's Air Division in France, I sometimes wonder how we all managed to survive in that French society. Few of us spoke any French, yet we seemed to cope. Of course, we all took French lessons and we tried (God knows, we tried) to learn the language. But somehow, just one word spoken in French could convince a French person that you had the whole vocabulary. It was far better, I discovered, to fake total dumbness no matter how excellent you thought your French – for it was never good enough. Seventy million language purists were quick to correct your every syllable.

It made learning the language doubly difficult. When I tried in my stumbling French to converse, say, with a shopkeeper, and if I paused, searching for a word – he immediately assumed I was German and switched to that ungodly, tongue-twisting language. Which made me hurry my thoughts and make a botch of everything.

The most annoying habit was the French insistence on correcting everything I said, no matter if it was understood or not. They all insisted that my accent be correct. This watchguard approach to their language seemed to apply to all segments of French society.

I walked down the street where I lived one nice afternoon to investigate buying a ton of coal from the local merchant. I wanted anthracite coal, and when I entered his coal-yard I was pleased to find that it contained nothing else. The merchant met me in his yard, his face, hands, and clothing covered with coal dust.

"*Oui, monsieur?*"

In my best accent (I had been practising as I walked down the street) I asked for a ton of anthracite. Something like, "*Une tonne anthracite, s'il vous plaît,*" came out of my mouth.

The merchant stared. "*Comment?*"

Mentally, I rehearsed the line and then phrased it in pure golden French.

Again. "*Comment?*"

Completely stupified by his reaction, I picked up a piece of coal and held it under his nose. "*Une tonne anthracite!*" I repeated. Not with any great confidence, but with greater volume. My mind continued to grapple with the problem. Surely, the word was spelled the same in French as in English? How could I be using the wrong word?

Suddenly, as though a battery had been switched on, the merchant smiled at me, his teeth looking like sticks of chalk inside his black face. "*Monsieur, c'est awn-thra-seat, ne pas anthracite.*"

"*Combien?*" I demanded, refusing to accept his French lesson. Giving him the money and my address, I left him standing in front of what looked like the world's total supply of anthracite. To this day I wonder what he thought I wanted in his coal-yard! Now that I know how to pronounce the word correctly, of course, I haven't found a conversation where it can be used. Which goes for 90 per cent of the French words I have memorized.

I have never been sure whether or not the French were, in their own way, having me on. I am afraid to examine the idea too closely, lest it be true. The small local store where I bought my house wine first started this train of thought.

Thumping down two empty wine bottles of a particular brand I liked, I addressed the store owner standing behind his counter. "*La même chose, s'il vous plaît.*"

"*Mais oui!*" he cried. And reaching below the counter he brought up two empty bottles – exactly like mine. "*Voilà, monsieur. Exactement.*" He stood there, grinning at me.

I eventually found the phrase "*Autre deux,*" or something equally asinine, hiding in my head. I was too confused, too addled, to know what I was saying. On reflection, I think that it was the shock of finding a Frenchman – especially a merchant – with a sense of humour, that undid my mind.

Everyone who has failed to master a second language needs experiences like that to fortify his strong belief that he could, if he really wanted to, easily speak another tongue. I know that it has been one of my major crutches over the years.

*   *   *

While stationed in France we had a guy called Morton in our section. When we'd go drinking with him in the local French cafés we could never understand why all the Frenchmen broke out laughing when we called him Mort.

We did learn, eventually, that *mort* in French means "dead."

*   *   *

When I had finished my operational tour in North Africa I was stationed at a Personnel Centre in Algiers. While we waited for a ship to return us to England we enjoyed the sand beaches and the fleshpots of the town.

One beautiful August night we were coming back to camp in a group. "Let's go for a swim in the sea!" someone yelled. We all sprinted for the water, shedding our clothes as we ran, and plunged happily into the waves. What we didn't know was that an oil tanker had been sunk just off shore that day . . . . When we surfaced we were covered with thick, stinky, black muck.

To make matters worse – it was past midnight. Which meant that the water was shut off until eight in the morning.

*   *   *

Four of us were on leave in Paris and doing what comes naturally to young, unmarried pilots. It was one solid round of nightclubs in

Pigalle, Montmartre, and Montparnasse. None of us could speak French – but we could all wave our arms to amplify the restaurant French we knew. We had a ball. We owned the town. When we weren't drinking we were watching floor-shows or entertaining the ladies sent up to our rooms by hotel waiters.

During the seven days we only had one minor scrape with the law. We were sitting at a sidewalk café recovering from a hard night, and we were eating oysters to get our strength back. One of our guys (always the joker) started throwing the oyster shells at passersby. So, naturally, we all joined in the fun. There was a hell of a row with police whistles blowing and waiters yelling and pedestrians threatening to kill us. As they should have done.

It took a *lot* of arm-waving – and lots of free drinks – to settle things down.

We left Paris the next afternoon, just at rush hour. Our joker friend was at the wheel. We were moving slowly down the Champs Elysées searching for a route south when we stopped at a red light.

Our driver turned to the guy who was in the front seat with him. "Look at that honey!" he said. Soon all of us were staring at a very beautiful girl, dressed as only the French girls dress.

"Reach out and pinch her ass," our driver told his companion. "Wait until the light turns green. As soon as you pinch her, I'll step on the gas."

It seemed like a great trick. Since we were only about a foot apart the girl had noticed the four of us leering at her, and she had turned her head haughtily away.

"Now!" yelled the joker, as the light turned green.

His buddy dutifully leaned out and gave the girl a pinch on the bottom. She let out a scream – we four laughed like mad – the crowd began yelling . . . . And instead of stepping on the gas our driver turned off the ignition key.

*   *   *

Anyone who lives in France for only a few years eventually meets the Gendarme – face to face.

The Gendarmes always lived up to the expectations I had founded on years of hearing and reading about them. They symbolized their country to foreigners in much the same way that

Scotland Yard and the Royal Canadian Mounted Police presented an image of their country. While stationed with the RCAF in Metz, France, I had many chances to put my well-held beliefs about Gendarmes to the test. Not by design, of course, but through those peculiar circumstances that afflict English-speaking people trying to live in France. I hasten to add that none of these confrontations ever diminished my high regard for this elite corps.

My belief in their invincibility was strengthened on the first occasion I drove an automobile in France. On that particular morning I came upon a six-way intersection jammed with traffic of all sorts, and in place of traffic lights, a uniformed figure was directing events. As was their wont, the French drivers were using their horns to tell the Gendarme on duty that they were impatient. When the honking had reached a crescendo, the Gendarme wheeled about smartly and marched, with rapid strides, across the intersection and into a bistro on the corner. Fascinated, I watched through the window as he pulled off his heavy gauntlets and, standing at the bar, knocked back a small glass of liquid. It was a cold day – so I figured that the drink was probably cognac. Refreshed, he strode briskly back into position and resumed his work. This, I thought with great admiration, was what the French meant by civilized behaviour!

A few months later, enroute to play golf in Luxembourg (which had the only golf course in our corner of the world) I got to meet a Gendarme for the first time. I had been pushing my old car to its maximum of 100 kilometres when I overtook another vehicle on a long, curving hill. Anxious to beat the forecast rain, I pulled around to pass – and the Gendarme came immediately into view.

His whistle sent me quickly to the side of the road where I parked and awaited his presence. I don't know why, but something made me turn to my three male companions and say, "No one speaks French." Since two of them spoke excellent French I expected a rejoinder. But they simply nodded although, for some reason, they seemed pleased.

The officer saluted as he got to my open window. "*Bonjour, monsieur,*" he said, drawing off his gloves. "*Les papiers, passeport!*"

"*Oui,*" I said, and reached into the glove compartment for the bundle of papers: insurance, licence, passport, and something called *carte grise*. I handed them to the officer and we all sat silent as he examined my official papers.

Then the Gendarme asked me – in French – how long I had lived in France. Forgetting my own counsel I replied, "*Quatre mois, monsieur.*"

I knew immediately that it had been the wrong thing to do. He began a long harangue in French which centred on my inability to drive and the unpardonable sin of passing a car on a hill. Then he asked where I was going.

I replied with a shrug and a lift of my hands, shaking my head to indicate that I didn't understand French.

"*Parlez-vous française?*" he asked.

"*Non.*" And again I shrugged.

Obviously baffled by the discrepancy between my earlier responses and my current denial of any knowledge of the language he told me that I *did* speak French.

"*Non, monsieur,*" I repeated.

The Gendarme leaned into the car, his face beginning to turn red, and asked each of my passengers if they spoke French. "*Vous! vous! vous!*" he barked, stabbing a finger at each one. Each in turn shrugged his shoulders and shook his head.

Straightening up, his emotions now clearly out of control, the Gendarme shoved my papers at me. "*Allez, allez!*" he roared. His arm swept forward, pointing up the road, and he yelled at the top of his voice, "*Allez!!*"

When our house was broken into it set the stage for another historic encounter with the Gendarmes. Amazingly, the police had arrested the burglar and recovered the loot that he had taken from our basement storage locker. The fact that we didn't know we had been robbed until the Gendarmes told us added to the bizarre episode. We immediately checked the locker, and found a broken padlock – but for the life of us we couldn't think of anything missing.

We were told to report to the local police headquarters to identify our goods. After a long search we found the office hidden away on the fourth floor of a nondescript stone building. We trudged up the stairs to find a Gendarme, cigarette pasted to his lower lip, accompanied by an Algerian assistant. They were rummaging through a pile of Christmas-tree lights, 200 pounds of potatoes I had recently purchased from a farmer, a bundle of old house dresses, and the back wheel of a bicycle. All I could remember owning was the large sack of potatoes. Hadn't I lifted them enough times getting them home from the farmer to know they were mine? Proving ownership was another matter.

Fortunately, my wife had made a determined effort when we first arrived in France to learn the language. She had attended classes each day with a perseverance I found awesome. While her vocabulary was very limited, she had overcome the fear of speaking French to the French. No mean accomplishment, I might add.

The wheel, the potatoes, and the Christmas-tree lights were held up in turn, and we were asked if they were ours. Somehow, my wife convinced the Gendarme that they were; but it seemed to take hours of hand-waving and many verbless sentences to satisfy him. The Algerian assistant was not allowed into the dialogue. His job, it seemed, was to hold up each article when it was indicated by an imperious wave of the Gendarme's hand.

The identification procedure continued until all that remained was the pile of dresses. The Algerian held up each dress in front of him, much like a person sizing a garment. They were much too large for him (and, indeed, were size forty-fours at the least). Until these dresses had come into view, my wife had been quite friendly. Now – as she recognized the old house-dresses her mother had sent for use as dusters – she seemed to lose her *savoir faire*.

The Gendarme asked my wife if they were hers.

I laughed. Which didn't seem to help the official inquiry. I could see the predicament my wife faced. How to convince the Gendarme that they were her dresses, but not *her* dresses? I thought I could read the messages her brain was flooding over her face. She found a lot of words like *maman, ancienne, grosse, chemise de maison, travail manuel* and such – but the French word for dusters evaded her.

When the Algerian had the temerity to hold one of the huge dresses before my wife, she dashed it aside. The Gendarme bowed to her ("*Pardon, madame!*") and threw a fierce glare at his assistant, who shrank back. Nevertheless, he persisted in going through the entire collection, and an approximate litany of these-are-my-mother's-old-house-dresses-that-she-sent-to-me-for-use-as-dusters continued to be butchered and quartered in the French language.

"Tell them you don't want them," I said. "Let's go." She would have none of it. Her blood was up and she was going to collect her goods despite the embarrassment.

Finally, the last dress was modelled. After signing our names a few times we were told, by a sweep of the Gendarme's arm, to take the loot away. It was then that I remembered we were four floors up – without, as usual, an elevator.

"The hell with it! I'm not going to carry those bloody potatoes down four flights of stairs. Look, we don't need this junk. Let's just leave it." I turned to leave. My wife hesitated and then began following me to the door.

At once, the office erupted in a babble of French. I could decipher none of it – but the message was plain. This is your junk. Get it to hell out of here.

My wife began gathering up the dresses, but I disagreed. "Come on," I urged. "Leave it!" Sensing my meaning, the Gendarme grabbed my arm and pointed to the potatoes. He was firing French at about 500 words a minute, as the Algerian moved to block the door. It was obvious that French law did not mean to be defeated.

I had planned on laughing all the way home in the car. I had planned on recounting (with appropriate gestures) how silly my wife had looked trying to explain that her dresses weren't *her* dresses. But my back was too sore from carrying those potatoes down four flights of stairs.

It destroyed my *jovialité*.

* * *

As the vanguard of our new NATO air arm, the RCAF did little to prepare us for life among our French hosts. This resulted in problems for both ourselves and the French.

In Metz I shared digs with another airman "on the economy," anxious to mix freely and learn something of our new home and its people. This was in direct contrast to most of the Canadians, who preferred to remain herded together.

Getting accepted into any level of French society was, we found, not easy. After some thought we decided that if we wanted to meet the French we would have to do it on their own territory. This, obviously, meant the local cafés. We decided to select one and try to blend into the atmosphere.

Madame Trapp, a handsome and gentle publican, gave us a small but firm smile as we entered Café Trapp and uttered the ritual greeting, "*Messieurs, dames.*" Nobody else smiled or acknowledged our presence. Silence fell over the tables; and the locals stirred only to mutter comments about *les américains* who had invaded their sanctuary.

We stood at the bar, our backs to the patrons, drinking our beer. After one drink we bid everyone *bon soir* and left. The eyes that had been riveted to the backs of our necks had left icy welts. Or so it felt.

Next day, at the same time, we returned to Madame Trapp's. We did this for several days until, slowly, the icicles melted. The first break came when the "character" of the group began exchanging small talk with us. Soon we were invited to join him for a *demi*, their term for a draft beer. He bought a round and we reciprocated. We tried never to break that arrangement, afraid that if we did we would become the Ugly Canadians – throwing our relative wealth around.

However, as time went by we began to feel guilty about accepting their hospitality, something they clearly could not afford. After some discussion we decided that we should take over the pub for an evening and stage a truly Canadian festival: a wiener roast.

We had difficulty translating our meaning since we were not only learning the customs of the country but the language as well. We said that true Canadiana called for a *fête des saucissons*. We explained to Madame Trapp that we would supply the food and drink if she could provide the pots and glasses. The French were fascinated, if uncomprehending, and made a special point of gathering early on the appointed Saturday evening.

Armed with hot dogs, buns, and many bottles of duty-free liquor, we descended upon the pub at the magic hour. We quickly found that rye whiskey was unfamiliar to our guests. "*Zut, alors!*" snorted Robert, an inveterate tosspot, who worked as a janitor in the area. "*Ce n'est rien du tout!*" he said, downing his first tumbler-full, waving away our warnings of disaster. The others, while more timid, were quite co-operative and very willing to try Canada's national drink.

In zero time the dancing started, and the normally vigorous local dances became absolute feats of gymnastics. We became so entranced with the wild gyrations that we almost forgot to cook the hot dogs.

"Quick!" I shouted to my buddy. "We'd better get the hot dogs going before they all pass out."

Even before we could fit the hot dogs into buns, Robert went missing. The more concerned among us began to worry that he had fallen into the canal. A search was started – but it was a short one. There lay Robert, spread-eagled in the middle of the street, dead to the world.

Fernand, a recruiting officer for the Foreign Legion, had been unmoved by Dien Bien Phu and a dozen early wars but he, too, had been seriously wounded by the Canadian Club. All six-feet-four of him was stiffened on a pub chair. A Metz detective who had cracked a delicate murder case (Mauricette vs. Le Boxeur, circa 1954) resembled a freshly murdered corpse himself. There were bodies sprawled all over the café. Those capable of speech were still declaring that rye whiskey was no stronger than canal water.

Our *fête des saucissons* – while perhaps not THE social event of the season – did provide a great opportunity for two Canadian airmen to, as it were, present their credentials. They were accepted with pleasure. And so were we.

Table Talk

I was enroute from NORAD Headquarters in Colorado Springs, heading back to 412 Squadron at Ottawa in a twin-jet Falcon transport. The jet stream was all screwed up that day, and instead of the expected tail winds we were bucking fairly heavy head winds. I decided that we would have to refuel before we could reach Ottawa, and chose a small civilian field in Indiana that was close to our track. We were a crew of three: two pilots and a crew man.

As I taxied into the ramp the usual race began among the fuel trucks to see which brand of aviation fuel I would choose. Three tankers lined up in front of our parked aircraft, and as I climbed out I pointed to the closest one. The other trucks drove off and the chosen one began the refuelling job.

Since we were in a hurry to get airborne again, the co-pilot hustled off to file a flight plan and check weather while the crewman and I chatted with the driver. As we stood there, we noticed a great long ribbon of green paper unwinding from the rear of the tanker. It began to snake its way across the tarmac as the breeze moved it around. Curious, I asked the driver what was happening. "Oh, those are your green stamps," he replied.

"What," I asked, "are green stamps?"

The driver gave me a funny look. "You know. Trading stamps. You get stuff for them at the store."

"We're going up to Canada," I said. "Those things won't be any use to us."

My crewman, who was tuned into the conversation, was quicker than I was. "What'll you give us for them?" he queried.

The driver paused for a moment and looked us over. "How about six cases of beer?"

It was a happy little crew who took off ten minutes later with six large cases of beer carefully stowed in the rear of the Falcon.

*　　*　　*

An RCAF pilot was spending his first weekend in wartime London. In order to do things right he had reserved a room at the Savoy, where he understood that things were always first class – if terribly English.

On his first evening he decided to dine in the hotel's rather sumptuous dining room. He was escorted to a table by the maître d' and a phalanx of hovering, solicitous waiters. A large, ornate menu was presented with appropriate flourishes, and a waiter suggested, rather imperiously: "You will have the soup, sir!"

The pilot, who had set up a secret rendezvous for the theatre that evening, declared that he was in a hurry and only wished the roast beef.

Obviously horrified, the waiter scurried away. The pilot could see him, out of the corner of his eye, talking and gesturing with the maître d'. In a few moments the maître d' approached the pilot's table to say: "Excuse me, sir. But may I say what a pleasure it is to have you dine with us this evening. I wonder, sir, if you appreciate that our specialty here at the Savoy is our soup. Everyone who stays with us always has soup for dinner."

The pilot, edgy about the passing time and fearing that he might miss the curtain, barked, "Just bring me some roast beef!"

In a few minutes a waiter appeared with a bowl of soup and began placing it on the table. "Look!" cried the pilot. "I'm in a hell of a hurry. I haven't *time* for soup. Just bring me the roast beef dinner!" Reluctantly, the waiter removed the soup and brought the dinner.

Sometime in the middle of the night, long after the pilot had gone to bed, a man in the next room suffered a heart attack. The hotel's doctor ordered him to remain in bed, and sent up two aides to administer an enema. This was intended to reduce fluids in the patient's body.

Unfortunately, the aides got into the pilot's room by mistake, and when they began to administer the enema he yelled, "Okay, okay! I give in!"

The next day, as the pilot was walking in Hyde Park, he met a squadron friend. They began chatting about London and how their leaves were working out. The pilot told his friend that he was staying at the Savoy – which was a new experience for him – and he asked if his friend had ever stayed there.

When his friend said no, he hadn't, the pilot told him: "Man, if you ever have dinner there just make damn sure you have the soup! Because if you don't they'll wake you up in the middle of the night and shove it up your ass."

*　*　*

On my first leave from Camp Borden I was lucky to catch a flight to Yarmouth – but unlucky in that I missed the return flight. I had to hitch-hike back with just ten bucks in my pocket.

I slept in a jail in Quebec City – and a jail in Cornwall – and when I reached Trenton I hadn't eaten in two days. They had some kind of hash for dinner, the kind I usually refused to eat. Without question, it was the best meal I ever ate in the air force!

*   *   *

When the North West Staging Route was in its heyday, RCAF personnel manned the small bases that stretched along its length. The bases were so isolated and removed from the mainstream of air force life that airmen had little to occupy their off-duty hours, especially during the long winter months.

The heart of each tiny station was the central power plant which supplied the vital heat and electricity. The operators of these power plants were universally characters of the first order. They loved engines more than life itself, and it was a rarity to find one of these units oily or greasy or ill-kept. Their sparkle reflected the commitment of a power plant operator who was proud of his title and his trade.

Still, the long Arctic months produced boredom in massive amounts, and even the most industrious operator couldn't escape its clutches for long. Adding to the interminable winter was the fact that not one drop of alcohol was allowed on the camp.

It was the combination of these conditions that led one artful operator to make his own brew – right in the powerhouse where few people ever ventured. As accomplices, he carefully selected a handful of trusty airmen. Together they gathered the necessary utensils and the ingredients to make a mash.

Day after day they transported pockets full of figs, prunes, dates, raisins, apricots, and other dried fruit to their cache in the power plant. When they were about to begin, Red, the power plant operator, decided that they should inform the RCMP Constable, just as a precaution.

The Mountie agreed to their plans but laid down three simple rules: don't tell others; don't give any to the natives working on the base; don't forget to invite the Mountie when the brew is ready.

The cornucopia of dried fruit was put into a borrowed kettle and properly covered with warm water. Then the pot was tucked into a warm corner behind the humming engines, safe from official, prying eyes.

In due course the bubbles arrived, and the fruit turned into a rolling stew. The thirsty airmen visited the pot frequently, only to be stood off by Red who kept insisting that it needed more time to mature. But before long, even Red thought it should be tasted – and he called the Mountie to help officiate. The murky liquid was drawn off and tasted. And tasted and tasted. In a few hours it had all been tasted.

Several natives were piled in a corner of the power plant. The mash kettle had been knocked over, and mash and squashed fruit were everywhere. The Mountie was bleeding profusely from cuts sustained when he had demonstrated that any size window can be punched out with a bare fist if one knows the correct technique.

Into this revelry walked the young Commanding Officer.

Red was arrested and charged on four counts of conduct prejudicial to good order and discipline, in that he did: steal fruit from the Mess hall; make illicit spirits; drink illicit spirits; and give illicit spirits to natives. The accused was shipped south to Edmonton for disposition of his case. But nothing was actually said to Red, and he wandered around for a month without receiving any sort of formal hearing.

One day during his wanderings Red bumped into a former CO with whom he was on friendly terms. The officer inquired what Red was doing in Edmonton, and Red told him his story. When the officer looked into the matter he could find no paper follow-up, so he decided to hear the case himself.

The charges were officially made and the sentence handed down: admonishment. No weaker sentence could be found in KR (Air). The sentence would be expunged from Red's records in six months time. A piece of cake.

It was the expunging process which brought this all to light. A personnel clerk, leafing routinely through the blue charge sheets of airmen, found Red's charges – which were long overdue for removal. But when Red was advised of this he objected vehemently.

"Leave the charge in there," he said. "That's the only bright spot on my northern career. It got me posted out of the north . . . . Besides," he added, "I wouldn't want to destroy such a spirited crime sheet and deny some future historian a chuckle."

* * *

It was Peg's birthday, and one of the young officers from the Signals Section had given her a bottle of rye whiskey. That evening, when we returned to barracks, four of us gathered together in the empty downstairs room. The lights were out and we were having a little nip in honour of the occasion when someone hissed: "Shhh! Somebody's coming!"

There was a flashlight probing about way down at the end of the room. Quickly, we stuffed the bottle under the mattress of the bed we were sitting on, and tried to keep as still as possible. But soon, the light grew closer, and the voice of a female Sergeant rang out in the silence. "Aha!" she cried. "Caught you in the act this time!"

The flashlight swept over us where we were crouching on the bunk – and suddenly, her manner underwent a complete change. She gurgled with laughter. "Golly!" she said. "I thought I had caught an airman in here entertaining his girlfriend. You must have thought I had lost my marbles, yelling at you like that. There are reports that some girls are bringing boys into this vacant room in the evenings and I was told to patrol here periodically."

After a few minutes of chatting the Sergeant went on her rounds – but we had lost our appetite for an illegal drink. It didn't taste that great, anyway! It was just exciting to be doing something we ought not to be doing.

* * *

The first time I flew home on leave was on a bitterly cold day in February. Before we boarded the Dakota scheduled flight, all the women were given cups of hot cocoa to warm them up. We weren't thirty minutes into the flight before we all had to answer nature's call. Another thirty minutes and we were in such anguish that our eyes were watering.

One of the girls timidly asked if there was a washroom on board. The Flight Sergeant turned bright red and asked us to follow him. Leading us to the back of the aircraft where our baggage was piled, he pointed to a hole in the floor.

We took turns – and those who were not engaged formed a protective semi-circle in front, just in case some unwary airman should decide to go. The old Dakota kept hitting air pockets and lurching around the sky and we bounced all over trying to use that john!

On subsequent flights, I refrained from drinking anything for hours before takeoff.

*　　*　　*

In the initial days of the Air Division Headquarters in Metz, there were few leisure-time facilities available on base. When they did become available the airwomen and airmen had become accustomed to finding their pleasures in the city fleshpots – often to the detriment of the Canadian image.

To break this habit, I was one of several airmen "asked" by the adjutant to organize some recreational pursuits to counteract the lure of the city lights. One of the brilliant solutions we arrived at (over copious quantities of brew) was the idea of holding a dance. Not any old dance but an Airmen's Ball, complete with large orchestra, decorations, fresh flowers, favours, a printed menu, and a grand entrance by the Air Officer Commanding and his wife. Top hole.

We were all anxious and nervous to put on a good show, especially with the AOC coming – but as the major-domo I was in an absolute sweat for weeks. On the day of the event I had my team cleaning and decorating. Never before in my young career had I undertaken such an awesome responsibility. As the work progressed, it called for many libations to soothe the nerves.

Late in the day, when all was in readiness, we closed the Mess until nine o'clock and repaired to my room for a final briefing and fresh drinks. As my team-mates finally withdrew from my room, I extracted a promise that they would awaken me if I hadn't appeared at the appointed hour. It was imperative, I told them, that I be there to greet the AOC and his guests. They told me to relax, and to have a short nap. They'd be on time to collect me and we could all go to the Mess together.

It didn't seem like a long nap before a heavy pounding started on my door. I rolled over to discover that it was eight o'clock. No time to spare! With the help of my buddies I showered, shaved, and got into my best uniform, and we all made a dash for the Mess.

As I tried to enter the building I was stopped by two Service Police and a French civilian guard.

"Sorry, the Mess is closed," offered the SP.

"Why?" I screamed in his face. "Look, here! I'm in charge. Why have you closed the Mess? The AOC and his guests will be here any minute!"

I was shouting at the top of my voice. (All I could imagine was that some great *mêlée* had broken out and the police had closed the place.) But the more I raved, the more bewildered the guards looked. I reminded them of the time, tapping my watch and displaying it to their startled faces. And then to my own startled face as I noticed the sun setting in the east . . . .

I turned to my colleagues for support and a possible explanation – only to find them rolling on the grass, drumming their heels in hysterical laughter. It was some time before I learned how they had crept through my bedroom window and reset my alarm clock.

I have never since slept that soundly.

* * *

Everyone who has suffered through a long, dull, and wine-filled Mess dinner, will sympathize with the need for a washroom when, finally, the dinner is over.

As one such dinner dragged to a close I made a quick sprint to the single toilet and locked the door behind me. I must have taken a long time, for there began to be a considerable banging and yelling at the door. Afraid of being trampled to death if I tried to walk out the door, I opened the window and climbed out. Since it was on the first floor there was no difficulty. I was soon back at the bar enjoying a beer – and watching the frantic line at the washroom door.

The line grew smaller as customers abandoned the idea of the washroom and went outside to find a hedge or a building. One of the guys happened to notice the open window from his vantage point behind the hedge. He climbed through the window and unlocked the bathroom door, expecting to be rewarded with congratulations. Instead, he was greeted with a barrage of insults and disparaging comments for taking so long.

* * *

I had hemorrhoids when I was stationed at Leeming in Yorkshire. They were very painful, but at first I preferred to put up with the

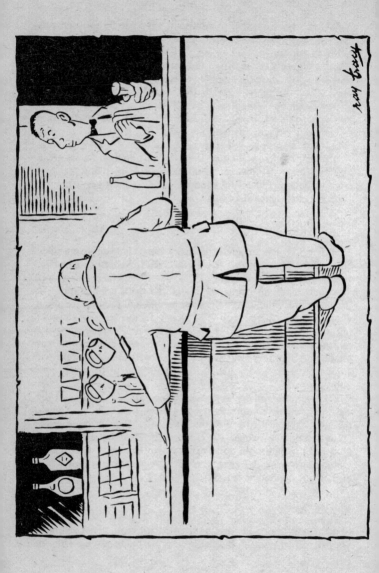

pain rather than go to the Medical Officer. After a couple of weeks the pain was so bad that I decided the doctor couldn't hurt me any more than I was already hurting – and I reported on sick parade.

I sat in the waiting room dreading my turn, visualizing the various operations that would be performed on me. Finally, I was shown into the doctor's office.

He examined me, then asked: "Do you drink beer?"

"No, sir," I replied.

"Well," the doctor said, "I want you to drink one pint of beer every day. Report back in seven days."

I don't think I've ever felt so wonderful. I simply floated out of his office, all my dreaded thoughts forgotten. Amazingly, the treatment worked! And I got to like beer so much I could even drink the NAAFI beer that had cork in it.

* * *

A Spitfire pilot engaged on ferrying duties flying new Spitfires from Gibraltar to Fez, in Morocco, always kept his friends in mind. Before each flight he removed all the ammunition from the gun ports and filled the space with sherry and other liquors.

He was never challenged by the Luftwaffe on these errands of mercy – but it is interesting to speculate that had he been bounced, he might have become the first Spit pilot to record a kill with a bottle of Dry Sack or a burst of Amontillado.

* * *

It was a bright, incredibly beautiful winter day when we steamed up the Firth of Clyde and docked at Greenock, Scotland. We stayed aboard all that day and night. Our ship was the *Empress of Scotland*, but underneath the paint you could still read *Empress of Japan*.

With the ship's engines idle we grew colder by the minute, so we were glad to disembark the next morning and board our troop train. A long delay when we reached Glasgow extended our trip, and we experienced our first blackout.

Early the following morning we arrived near Liverpool at the RAF Posting-In Depot. A place called West Kirby. Here we were dumped into freezing Nissen huts. The beds had no blankets – and there was only the wire springs and a rock-hard thing called a bolster for a pillow. While we were bitching and griping, a Corporal stuck his head through the door and told us that the Mess was open. Since we were all starving we stampeded to the Mess, only to find ourselves at the end of a long queue.

Eventually, we were each given one fritter-like object in the middle of our plate. (I have never figured out what it actually was.) Since we were in an RAF Mess we were without knife, fork, or spoon. These had not yet been issued to us. We managed, however, to down our fritter by hand – and in our starved condition it tasted wonderful! Even though it wasn't very big.

As soon as I had wolfed my fritter I got quickly back into line for another. But all I got from the cook was a caustic comment: "Who do you think you bleedin' well are? Oliver Twist?"

Air Force Blues

When unification of the forces became the prime concern of the military, senior officers at Ottawa elicited the support of the Operational Commanders by asking for their advice on various aspects of unification. Commanders were aware that non-support would adversely affect their careers – and so most were not willing to "rock the boat."

However, when we were asked our opinions about the colour and design of a new common uniform to replace our air force blue, Headquarters received some startling ideas. They were most upset to receive my suggestion that the new uniform should be white with small, red, maple leaves dotted all over it. In short order, a senior officer called to point out the error of my ways.

* * *

We were headed for Montreal aboard a C-119 from 435 Squadron, carrying a mixed load of people and cargo from Goose Bay. One of those passengers was a Captain in the United States Air Force who had gone mental while stationed at Goose. He was now being flown out to hospital.

It was a hell of a dark night with many thunderstorms enroute; and of course the C-119 wasn't a pressurized aircraft and couldn't climb above the weather. We were all bouncing and banging around when the USAF Captain came onto the flight deck to see the pilot.

He said he had just received a message from God that we were about to crash. To which the skipper replied: "I'm sure glad someone is receiving messages. Our radio officer hasn't heard a thing in the last hour."

* * *

On our trip overseas aboard the *Empress of Scotland* we headed south out of Halifax on our own, while a large convoy headed northeast, shadowed by a U-boat pack. We had about 2,800 RCAF, RAF, and Norwegian aircrew packed on board. I was a navigator, newly graduated from No. 1 Air Observers School at Malton, Ontario; and during the voyage I hung around with the guys I had trained with at Malton.

We crossed the Atlantic at twenty-nine degrees north latitude –

and on the fourth day out, somewhere west of Gibraltar, our group spotted a Liberator aircraft in the distance. After about twenty minutes of watching the Liberator cruising around, the ship's horn sounded. We were all ordered below because "an unidentified aircraft" had been discovered in the vicinity.

A short time later we were allowed back on deck, where we began to read the Aldis Lamp signals from the aircraft. Then the Captain ordered the aircraft to switch to code – since his passengers were all aircrew and could read the messages!

I have always wondered what he thought we might do with the innocuous information we were intercepting.

* * *

One of our groundcrew from out west was an aero-engine mechanic, and he decided to wash his uniform in aviation gas in order to get the grease out of it. He was merrily washing the uniform in a couple of gallons of gas when he was detected. His punishment was seven days Confined to Barracks and fourteen days Kitchen Police.

Part of his duty was to scrub the hangar floors with hundreds and hundreds of gallons of aviation gas in preparation for a Royal Visit.

* * *

As a Station Warrant Officer I had more than my share of parading defaulters before Commanding Officers. "March in the accused!" still rings in my ears. As does, "Left, right, left, right, prisoner halt!" There, hatless, and at full attention, the accused faced the Station Commander to receive his sentence.

One CO I served under had a very unique way of emphasizing his remarks to a prisoner. I didn't immediately recognize it as a trick – but I certainly remember the first time I marched a prisoner before him.

When we had all halted in front of the CO's desk, the charge was formally read out. The prisoner was then asked if he would accept the CO's punishment or elect a higher court. If the prisoner decided that he had more chance of a light sentence by accepting

the CO's findings he chose that route, and was lectured and sentenced on the spot.

This particular day the prisoner elected to receive the CO's punishment, and the CO started in on him.

"What in hell do you mean, young man, by going absent without leave?" he bellowed, and at the same time he slammed shut a drawer of his desk with a tremendous crash.

I jumped about a foot.

"Who in hell do you think you are that you can walk out any time you feel like it?" Smash went another drawer. "In this man's air force you do as you are told. Do you understand?" *Bang, boom* went another drawer. One of the large, multiple ones.

I glanced at the prisoner and he was white as a sheet. He looked like he expected the next bang to come from a gun. The sentence was awarded with the slamming of the last drawer and I marched a rather wobbly prisoner out to serve his sentence.

* * *

We had a crusty old gentleman for a Commanding Officer. One of the original members of the RCAF, he nearly had apoplexy when the first WD's were posted onto his station. In any situation, his bark was just as famous as his bite.

One day I was confined to hospital when he made his rounds with the Medical Officer. In his caustic manner he asked, "What's wrong with this man?"

"I don't know, sir," replied the MO. "It's either poison oak or poison ivy."

The CO retorted: "You don't know? And *you* are the Medical Officer?"

With that he stomped off, not even bothering to ask how I was feeling. (Incidentally, it was the poison ivy that grew along the perimeter fence.)

* * *

We were a bunch of aircrew hopefuls at Lachine, waiting for postings to Initial Training School. Lachine was a short tram ride from Montreal – so life wasn't all that bad. The only real problem we had was the lack of something to do while we sweated out our postings.

Then some genius decided to sod the entire station, and he began looking for volunteers to lay sod. A deal was struck. In return for volunteering we would get a forty-eight hour pass every weekend. Such an offer was too good to be true and we all volunteered.

All went well until the first Friday, when our drill Corporal informed us: "Sorry, no forty-eight hour passes." We replied in one voice, as though we had rehearsed it for a long time: "Sorry, no more sodding."

It appeared that the Corporal had a mutiny on his hands. Off he went to arrange for the Commanding Officer to deal with it. We were then paraded to the drill hall where the CO would speak to us.

When we were all properly marshalled in the drill hall, the CO appeared on the platform. "Are all of you aircrew?" he asked. Our response was a roar of, "Yes, *sir!*" The CO was a World War One pilot and our response brought a smile to his face. He told us to pick up our passes in the morning and dismissed the parade.

We were at Lachine for another four weeks, and we got to enjoy laying sod – not to mention the forty-eight hour passes. But in those four weeks none of us ever saw the hapless Corporal.

* * *

As a clerk, in a Command Headquarters I don't wish to identify, I worked on the top floor of the building. This was the personnel branch, and there was a substantial paper flow through our offices at all times.

One day a memo arrived at my desk splashed with green ink. The ink identified it as coming from the pen of the Air Officer Commanding. (His writing was indecipherable, but his secretary always helped by typing out the message.) This particular memo outlined the AOC's wish to send a Christmas card to all his Allied colleagues in the NATO forces. It was, he said, an open list, and all officers were commanded to append additional names and addresses. All the names gathered to that point were attached to the memo on a large sheaf of paper.

Anything written in green ink got immediate attention, and the

Christmas list was quickly dealt with by most of the "P" branch officers. Then, horror of horrors, the list went missing! The AOC's notes to expedite the list grew more and more impatient as Christmas approached. Everyone was frantically searching everywhere – but it simply was not in our branch.

After some ten days, all hope of ever finding the Christmas list appeared gone forever. It was then that I received a personal package in the mail from Canada. Curious as to why I would get such a personally-addressed parcel from Air Force Headquarters, I took it to my office. It was lunch time, and for the moment the office was empty. When I opened the parcel and saw the contents my stomach felt like ice-cold ginger ale. A note fell out of the wrappings: "This arrived at AFHQ/DPA records clipped to some personnel files. I thought you might like to slide it back into the system personally."

What a break! What thinking!

I quickly found a bunch of files on someone's desk (a pile likely to be acted upon after lunch) and I slid the bundle, green side up, into the pile near the top. Then I nonchalantly resumed my duties, thumbing through some personnel files.

Within minutes a shout of disbelieving joy rang out. "I found it, I found it! I found the missing Christmas card list!" Instantly, a mob of officers gathered to inspect the miraculous find.

Christmas, I like to think, was merry that year all over NATO. I know mine was.

*　*　*

We were airborne in a C-119 over Lake Superior, enroute from Trenton to Winnipeg with a maximum load of filing cabinets.

It was a beautiful summer day and I had the aircraft on automatic pilot. I had placed a clipboard on the pedestal, and was playing knock-rummy with my co-pilot to pass some hours away. At the time, my co-pilot was suffering from a severe case of hemorrhoids. He was in so much agony that he delayed and delayed his trips to the bathroom. As a result, he was given to passing foul gas.

As I was dealing the cards he suddenly let go, and I swung around quickly to open the side window in order to air out the cockpit. I had a radio facility chartbook hanging on a spring-type clip on the window, and as I jerked open the window out went the book. The next thing we knew the engine on that side was starting to run down!

The flight engineer thought that the book had gone into the carburettor air intake. He was right. When we checked, the book was half in and half out and shredding to pieces in the slipstream.

We began losing altitude, and I knew we couldn't maintain height on one engine. I altered course for Houghton, Michigan, which was the nearest airfield, and wondered how we could lighten our load. There was a Flight Lieutenant escorting the filing cabinets on their trip, and I called him up to the flight deck.

"How many of those filing cabinets can we ditch?" I asked.

"Why do you think I'm wearing this .38 revolver?" he replied. "All those cabinets contain top secret material. If you're going to drop them in Lake Superior, you'd better drop me first."

We made it into Houghton on a straight-in approach, clearing the fence by inches. It took three days to pick the paper out of the nooks and crannies of the engine. When we examined the carburettor intake screen it looked like a rat's nest, completely blocked by shredded paper.

I decided that my official explanation should adhere to the truth (except, of course, when it came to the reason why the window was opened): "The captain dropped his pen and as he straightened up from retrieving it, he inadvertently caught the epaulet of his flying suit in the window release handle . . . ."

The Squadron Commander went up for three hours to try to duplicate our feat. For some reason he never succeeded.

*   *   *

A very senior officer was attending the court martial of an air gunner who was being tried on a charge of Lack of Moral Fibre: a refusal to continue flying on operations.

As the trial progressed the very senior officer became more and more disgusted. He ventured the observation that when he was flying DH-7's in World War One, he had never known a moment's fear.

Whereupon the defence counsel suggested: "Sir, that may be so, but we are dealing here with a sensitive boy with imagination."

*   *   *

There was a rear gunner friend of mine who remarked: "I never like to ask a navigator for the time. He'll look at his watch, which he wears under his wrist, and say, 'In ten seconds it will be exactly thirteen hundred hours, twenty-six and a half minutes.' When all I want to know is whether it's before or after lunch!"

* * *

When our course arrived for guard duty at No. 36 Service Flying Training School in Swift Current, Saskatchewan, we found that the station was still under construction. There was no water and no sewers. Our toilet was an outhouse with six holes located about seventy-five feet from our barracks block.

It was the middle of February, and the temperature was around thirty below zero. The seventy-five feet to that outhouse was a real character builder – and of course the visits to it were kept as short as possible. There was more than one airman who threatened to set the outhouse on fire so that it would be warmer sitting there.

When the station was completed, the place where the outhouse stood became the Officers' Mess.

* * *

One of the airmen in the propeller shop was found sleeping in a chair by the Commanding Officer. As the NCO in charge I was called in to observe him sleeping. He was formally charged with sleeping on the job – which was a new one on me since I thought that only applied to guard duty. Besides, it was just possible that the man might have inhaled too many paint fumes.

When the charge was taken, I was asked by the CO if the man had been sleeping. "I don't know, sir," I replied, "since I'm not a doctor. But the airman may have inhaled some paint."

The charge was dismissed. I later told the airman to find a better place to sleep.

* * *

Looking back, it seems to me that I spent the greater part of the war either trying to get clearance from old units or trying to get bedding from new ones. I had two weeks leave each year, of course

233

– and I spent a certain amount of time on my knees begging weekend passes so that I could visit my dying uncle. But mostly, as I remember, my major campaigns were those during which I was either stumbling out of a camp or crawling into one, locked in pitched battle with three duffle-bags (two larger than I, and one slightly smaller, but twice as crafty). What appeared from camp to be an approaching dust storm often turned out to be me, inching along with my three duffle-bags, my posting papers clutched between my teeth. I was too humble in rank to merit Motor Transport.

My rank and trade (General Duties) implied a mental capacity roughly comparable to that of a semi-trained ox, and MT dispatchers seemed to presume that I had a similar ability to haul heavy loads over long distances. If they were in a beneficent mood, say on Christmas Day, or if they were expecting their discharge, they would let me ride with the garbage run. It always sobered me, when posted, to leave camp with the garbage – bouncing up and down with the cans on the back of the truck. It was the same riding into a new station with a truckload of toilet tissue and other dispensables. Those were the times that made me wonder whether I was vital to an Allied victory.

Upon my arrival at a new unit, while I was standing dazed in the middle of camp, surrounded by my duffle-bags, the first official ceremony was for a Service Policeman to come along and bawl me out for not wearing the dress of the day. It was my experience that no two camps ever agreed on the same dress of the day. One camp would insist on you wearing a tie, another would drag you feet first in front of the station Warrant Officer if you had anything around your neck but a dirty ring. At one unit, everybody would be pounding about in shorts. At another, shorts would get you thirty days and a long talk with the Padre.

After being told off by the Service Policeman, my next move was to find the Orderly Room and report in: a routine that required worrying the duffle-bags down numerous corridors, then standing waiting for somebody to look happy to see me. Nobody ever looked happy to see me.

In fact, nobody could see me at all. I'd stand at the counter, teeth flashing out of my sweaty, dust-lined face, and the clerks would never even notice me. If they happened to look up from their work of typing sheets and tearing them up, they would stare

right past me, or through me, until I developed the gnawing suspicion that I had somehow become transparent.

Only when a clerk had to come to the counter anyway (to spit or something) was I handed a reporting-in form – to be made out in triplicate and handed back with my right eye as a token of good faith.

At the station Warrant Officer's office I was welcomed without enthusiasm. Aside from going red in the face and ordering somebody to open a window, the officer himself would have nothing to do with me. An underling would study a map of the camp and, having determined which barracks was farthest away, would assign me to it.

Usually, before I could start my safari towards this remote hutment, dinner time arrived, and people left their posts at a gallop. Desperately hungry but ignorant of the location of the Mess, I would abandon my duffle-bags and lope after someone with the same rank I had. Sometimes this person proved to be running for a bus or the lavatory or some similarly foodless objective, and I'd have to find another runner and swing in behind him.

After dinner I usually experienced some difficulty in obtaining bedding. During the day it was a relatively simple matter to track down the duty storekeeper. It required only a few hours at the most and provided an excellent opportunity to look over the entire station. On some of the more progressive stations where they had a golf course for the personnel, I could also look for him out on the green. Or he might be hiding at the bottom of the swimming pool. But – at least in the daylight – the new arrival had a fair chance of getting his bedding.

At night, however, it was necessary to conjure up an evasive sprite called the Orderly Corporal. It was characteristic of all units that the Orderly Corporal, immediately upon donning his armband, turned into a will-o'-the-wisp that could be found only with the aid of bloodhounds. Since most units couldn't provide a pack of bloodhounds out of non-public funds, the bedding hunter had to lie in wait along a certain path which Orderly Corporals were known to frequent. Notably, the one to and from the Wet canteen. Orderly Corporals and Orderly Sergeants shared a common weakness. They were unable to hide very long without stealing stealthily down to the beer-hole to drink.

Once I had the Orderly Corporal cornered I asked for some bedding. Now, if there was anything one of those creatures hated, it was giving you bedding. You got the impression that they wove the blankets themselves and received the linen from the hands of their old Irish mother, just before she passed away.

But after I had picked up the bedding from the road where the Corporal had thrown it, heaped it on top of my duffle-bags, and pointed myself in the direction of the distant barracks block, I began to feel that I was once more a baptized member of the station's personnel.

I could look forward to making new friends. I could look forward to learning new tricks of the trade. I could look forward to another posting.

*   *   *

Our Base Commander had a sign erected at the Orderly Room entrance, of which he was inordinately proud. It read: "Through these doors pass the best people in the world." But due to some construction going on, another sign underneath read: "Use south entrance, please."

Above and Beyond

The RCAF's monumental task of photographing all of Canada from the air – for the purpose of mapping the country – began almost as soon as the air force was formed in 1924. Initially, the only aircraft available were the old flying boats with their open front cockpits. The crewmen had to hand-hold the large, ungainly cameras, attempting to keep them steady as the flying boats bumped along. Things remained much that way until the war ended and larger, more efficient aircraft became available.

In 1946, the RCAF set about the job in earnest. And by 1948 three squadrons were operating out of Rockcliffe: numbers 408, 413, and 414. Lancaster, Canso, Dakota, Mitchell, and Norseman aircraft were all used. Recruiting was opened up, and many wartime aircrew who were bored with civilian life returned to the smells and sounds of the old Lancasters and Dakotas, helping to fill in Canada's blank map sheets.

The photo season extended from April until October. This was considered a relatively ice-free period, although Arctic lakes and rivers were often ice-bound until late July. The biggest consideration was cloudy weather, which prevented the cameras from recording ground detail.

Each spring the squadrons left Ottawa and headed north for spots such as Churchill, The Pas, Norman Wells, Dawson Creek, Yellowknife, Sawmill Bay, Resolute Bay, or wherever a likely airfield presented itself. Here detachments were set up, and here the crews remained until fall arrived. The Canso and Norseman aircraft operated mostly from lakes and rivers on a variety of related tasks, such as geodetic surveys. With ground bearings, they fixed points of reference for tying the aerial photos into the national grid. The Canso crews also did the bullwork of installing Shoran crews in the most godawful spots in Canada. These were usually located high on some forlorn peak in the Yukon, and every pound of cargo had to be carried up those steep mountains on their backs.

All of the detachments were in remote areas where the crews had to rough out their summers – but the Lancaster detachment at Yellowknife had more variety. Here the crews had access to a town that never slept. The bars were open twenty-four hours a day, seven days a week. The basis for the town was three active goldmines, and the miners gave the town colour and character. The air force always entered a baseball team in the local league, and the games started sharp at ten o'clock each night under a full, Arctic sun.

When the weather was suitable for flying, aircraft stayed airborne until the fuel gave out. Twelve-hour flights were common in the Lancasters – and those days had to be experienced to be believed. The aircraft were unpressurized, and oxygen masks were compulsory since the photo was always done at 20,000 feet. There was no galley on board, and only one regular pilot's seat. The two pilots rotated every two hours for the flying was most demanding: no more than fifty feet plus or minus height allowance and no more than one degree on each side of your compass heading. It was like ploughing a field. Straight and level. Up and down photo lines that were 200 miles long. The roar of the Merlin engines prevented any communication except by intercom.

Weather was the one constant factor on everyone's mind: would tomorrow be a cloud-free day, or would the clouds roll in and prevent aerial photography? Everyone erred on the side of bad weather and kept the parties going far into the night – only to find the dawn bright and cloud-free. Oh, Jesus. The pounding heads, the pounding engines, the insufferable oxygen masks. Back and forth on the photo lines, hour after long hour. Watch your height, watch your heading. And look, look, look for clouds. Cheers came from the crew as they spotted the first little white puffs, like popcorn bursting in a blue sky. Only then would you feel you might just survive to have a hair of the dog.

The photo squadrons were, in essence, extending Canada's northern frontier – challenging the existing geography. Crews discovered many pieces of Canada never previously recorded. They found the entire western shore of Hudson Bay to be incorrectly placed on our charts. They discovered that the North Magnetic Pole was not where scientists thought it should be. And they found a giant crater in northern Quebec.

In the summer of 1950, the Iron Ore Company wanted to open its newly-discovered Schefferville iron ore deposits. The trouble was that Schefferville lay 350 miles north of Sept Iles, and there were no roads, no railways, and no maps of that area. In order to build a railroad through that inhospitable wilderness, maps were a vital first requirement. In less than thirty days the photo squadrons had mapped every inch of the route, and steel was being laid.

There were many "wartime" characters on the photo crews – guys who hadn't heard that the war had ended and were still drinking, wenching, and flying as if there were no tomorrow. Eventually, of course, the guys got married and began families. The peacetime tempo took over and the wild ones were weeded out.

"Dewey" was one of the lads who turned a lot of hair grey. A Pathfinder navigator with two tours of bomber operations and the Distinguished Flying Cross, he had what is politely termed a drinking problem. After many disastrous airborne failures he was grounded and given an administrative job. His response to this was to go out and buy another hat. One hat he kept in his office, the other he kept on his head. When someone inquired, "Where's Dewey?" the answer was sure to be, "Oh, he must be around here somewhere. His hat's in his office." Dewey was more than likely on his third pint in the local tavern when the question was asked.

Another favourite character was also a navigator. He became bored with flying, and to amuse himself, put two girls to work for him on the streets of Hull. These supervisory duties kept him occupied into the wee hours so that his appearance in the morning degenerated. His uniform and general unkempt looks got so disreputable that they finally drew down the ire of a senior officer. After a loudly worded exchange the navigator was retired.

Hardly a week later he returned to the Mess to visit his pals. He drove up in a new Cadillac convertible, nicely appointed with three of his employees.

* * *

In those postwar photo days of the RCAF, our Dakota aircraft weren't pressurized. Since we operated at 20,000 feet, oxygen and oxygen masks were vital to the safety of the crew. The captain always called when climbing through 10,000 feet to tell us to turn on our oxygen.

This particular day the skipper called, "Oxygen on!" and all the crew but the navigator responded. After making several calls to the navigator without receiving any answer, the skipper handed over control of the Dak to the co-pilot and, strapping on a portable oxygen bottle, made his way back to the navigator's position.

There he found the navigator, head down on his map table. A

half empty bottle of whiskey was beside his head along with a crudely-lettered sign reading: "Do you have an appointment?"

* * *

We were flying geodetic survey operations out of Rockcliffe airbase in 1946. The squadron operated with Canso and Norseman water aircraft, and that summer we established our base camp in northern Quebec.

One of the Norseman pilots was much older than the rest of us. He seemed to me to be at least 100 years old. I never knew his first name, but I always referred to him as "the old gent." He got bushed as soon as he was ten miles north of Ottawa.

The first thing the old gent did that summer was get lost in a Norseman – just after we opened camp. When I heard about his situation I was with the supply Canso at Bagotville. We took off with a full load of fuel and headed out to look for him. But we ran into a fierce electrical storm and had to return to Bagotville. Then the weather socked in, and it was three days before we reached the base camp and began our search.

I made a guess that the old gent would be down somewhere northeast of base camp – and sure enough, ten minutes after take-off we spotted the Norseman. It was only thirty miles from camp. Now that area had some of the largest lakes in Quebec. But where was the old gent? On the smallest damn lake in the whole of Canada.

There was no way of landing a Canso in that puddle, which meant we had to return to base and try to rescue him with another Norseman aircraft. Everyone was highly pissed off at his stupidity so we decided to give him a scare. We flew right past him, giving no sign of recognition.

The next thing we saw was the First of July. The old gent was firing flares in all directions. After a while we turned and flew back over him, waggling our wings as we headed for camp.

That evening I saw him sitting by himself near his tent, and I went over and asked why he was so sad. I figured he should be overjoyed with his rescue.

"I know, kid," he said to me. "I'm just mad at myself. I sat there on that damn little lake for three days trying to think of some way to light a signal fire. Since I don't smoke I didn't have a

match, so I just sat there . . . ." He pointed past me to the north-east and yelled, "And look at that goddamned fire, now!"

I looked around to see a pall of smoke covering the horizon. The fire, started by the flares the old gent had fired at us, burned for days.

Some weeks later we moved our base camp to an unnamed and unmapped lake in the Ungava area. It just so happened that on the day we landed on that lake, the old gent's first child was born. He suggested that we name the lake for his son.

In the fall, when we returned to Rockcliffe, I submitted my maps with all the newly-discovered and newly-named geographical features. Unfortunately, the government had changed the policy that year and they would only accept the names of deceased persons. When I tried to explain the new policy to the old gent, he said, "That's a bunch of crap!" He never did stop asking, "When are you going to get that goddamned lake named for my son?"

The following summer, as we were preparing to head north, the old gent broke the news that he had taken a geology course during the winter months. "We are going," he told me, "to make our fortune." He wanted me to keep a close eye out for gold, since it was plentiful where we were headed. "Also," he added, "watch for blue clay." When I looked puzzled, he said, "Christ, kid, don't you know nothing? Blue clay means diamonds!"

As the season wore on I forgot about the old gent's geology lessons. Then one day, in Yellowknife, I was visiting one of the gold-mines. I asked my guide for a piece of ore and he gave me a chunk about as big as my fist. When I got back to camp I gave it to the old gent, saying that I had struck gold and our fortunes were made. He grabbed the ore and fled into his tent to run a test with his portable gold-testing kit.

Some time later he emerged from his tent and handed me the rock. "Hell, kid," he lamented, "it's no good. It's not even the right kind of rock."

Later that summer I managed to obtain some blue dye, and I coloured a ball of clay, figuring to have some fun with the old gent. When I gave it to him he went crazy with excitement, saying that it was the exact clay that diamonds came from and we should stake our claims right away. I managed to stall him for a few days until he had thoroughly examined the clay ball. That brought our mining partnership to a sudden halt.

At the end of that summer I lost touch with the old gent – and it was twenty years before I ran into him again. I had landed at a western RCAF station, and as we taxied in to the hangar I noticed a guard of honour and a parade forming up. As we swung onto the ramp and parked, part of the formation suddenly made a dash for our aircraft.

I stepped out to find that the group was led by a very red-nosed senior officer who, on closer inspection, proved to be the old gent! As he came to a puffing halt in front of me, I said, "Hey, old buddy, I knew you'd be overjoyed to see me, but this is too much. Dismiss the troops."

For a brief second I thought he was going to have a stroke right on the spot. His face went purple as he started yelling: "Get that fucking aircraft the hell out of here! The AOC is landing in five minutes for his annual inspection and you're in his parking spot!"

That was the last time I ever saw the old gent.

*   *   *

In my Communications Section at Goose Bay in the 1960s I had a Flight Sergeant with a delightful sense of humour. This was an asset deeply appreciated at any remote base.

At Goose Bay, the arrival of any aircraft was an event. It didn't matter whether it was Air Canada or a service aircraft, everyone who had the time wandered down to the flight line to be on hand. It reminded you of the old days, when the train pulled into the depot. It was the thing to do.

On this occasion a blizzard was blowing, and the usual crowd, including the Padre, was on hand as a Vanguard circled overhead. We couldn't see the aircraft because of the swirling snow and low cloud, but we could hear it from time to time as it attempted landings. It was making Ground Control approaches, hoping to find a momentary improvement in conditions which would allow the pilot to see the end of the runway. Our Flight Sergeant was aboard the Vanguard, returning from Montreal. Eventually, to everyone's relief, the pilot got the aircraft on the ground and taxied in.

We were all sympathizing with the passengers over their "hairy ride" when the Padre remarked to the Flight Sergeant that he must have had a stressful time. The Flight Sergeant agreed. It was a button-snapper, he said, and he had been so worried that he had almost done something religious.

The Padre was somewhat suspicious, but his curiosity made him ask what it was. "Padre," said the Flight Sergeant, "I almost took up a collection."

*　　*　　*

When we were stationed at Goose Bay, a United States Air Force Albatross of the Fifty-Fourth Air Rescue Squadron had occasion to land at one of the isolated coastal settlements along the Labrador coast. The crew had to remain overnight, and in the morning they found the Albatross frozen solidly in the ice. It took a great deal of time and effort by a lot of people to get the aircraft free and into open water. Needless to say, our USAF friends took a lot of ribbing over the incident. But it wasn't long before they got their own back.

In early December, the ice on Terrington Basin was deemed thick enough to support the ice-fishing huts which were a part of our winter recreation program. A bulldozer began to move the huts onto the ice. Suddenly, over deep water, there was an ominous crack – and the bulldozer sank to the bottom of the basin. The operator had bailed out in time but the station was left with two problems: getting the bulldozer out; and explaining the incident to Air Transport Command Headquarters.

A few weeks later, at a joint USAF-RCAF all-ranks Christmas gathering, the USAF Commander announced that he had a presentation to make to our Commanding Officer. He presented a foot-square block of ice. In the middle of it was frozen a tiny bulldozer.

*　　*　　*

In direct contrast to the Maritime provinces, the west coast of Canada has always been a mysterious place for the majority of Canadians. It was even more so back in 1939, when the war began.

The RCAF had one airbase when hostilities broke out. It was located at Jericho Beach in Vancouver. Vancouver Island, the

Queen Charlotte Islands, and the hundreds of miles of rugged coastline stretching north had none. So the government got busy and began building a string of defence sites and airbases. While some of them were full airbases complete with land runways that had been hacked from virgin timberland, others were craggy coastal bases for flying boats and seaplanes. Still others were radio and radar bases. Stuck on tiny, rocky islands, mountainous peaks, or deep fiords along the coast, they were accessible only from the sea. The airmen who manned these choice locations had plenty of beautiful scenery. In fact it was endless – and they had it all to themselves.

When the war was over almost all of these Pacific marine bases were closed and turned over to War Assets Corporation. But there was a period following VJ Day, before the wreckers arrived, when these stations were fully operational in the military sense, although they had no military value.

One of these was situated on "Insect Island." It was a lonely weather and radio station manned by members of the RCAF, and it lay a short distance from an inlet in a remote area of the coast. The island was fairly small but it had a snug harbour where flying boats and float planes could ride at anchor or tie up to the jetty. In common with similar bases on the coast, this one was quite big. It had a parade square, drill hall, guard house, motor compound, fire hall, bakery, powerhouse, and fuel dump. It had Mess halls, barracks, administration buildings, canteens, maintenance buildings, and fences. And a flagpole complete with painted rocks.

The heart of the station – the radio shack and antennae towers – was situated in the central part of the island, and could be reached by a drive of some two miles along a road that was part corduroy and part planking. Transportation was provided by a blue jeep, a large yellow 4WD dump truck, and a Caterpillar tractor, camouflaged in khaki brown. About seventy-five airmen kept the station at a high state of readiness.

At the end of the war the entire staff was abruptly transferred away and replaced by two airmen on caretaker duties. They were to oversee things until the base and hundreds of others just like it could be properly disposed of by War Assets. The two airmen assigned to this "holding" operation were former aircrew Flying Officers recently returned from overseas duty and now reduced in rank to Corporal.

I met these two Corporals when I was stationed at Western Air Command in Vancouver and they arrived there on a quick visit. I was very anxious to meet them, for their weekly reports had been coming in alternately signed Corporal Brown for Corporal Smith, NCO in charge, or Corporal Smith for Corporal Brown, NCO in charge. It was an interesting solution to the problem of who was in command – but not half as interesting as the hurried visit to Head-quarters.

Corporals Smith and Brown were in Vancouver to book a night-club act for their "club" at Insect Island. They said they didn't need an elaborate act and could probably get by with a piano player who could double as a singer. Someone who wouldn't mind helping them out during the week when business at the club was slow.

My question to them was: What club?

It slowly became apparent that in spite of its remote location, Insect Island was not as lonely a place as it might first appear. The British Columbia fishing fleet appreciated the snug harbour and safe moorings, and the restless fishermen, like sailors everywhere, were always anxious to go ashore when in harbour. They enjoyed the hot showers and the chance to sleep in a comfortable bed. There was always laundry to be done in the automatic washing machines, and time for a game of pool in the recreation hall or a game of inter-boat basketball.

Facilities of the canteen (the club) were available to members and their guests after the games or on the weekends. Fresh bread for the fleet was made in the bakery. Meat and produce was stored in the large, walk-in lockers and freezers. These services were much appreciated by the fishermen, for the Corporals – pointing out that the overhead was low – didn't charge them much. As a further inducement, they readily accepted fish when cash was in short supply.

A driving school was established under the direction of a Chief Driving Instructor (who alternated with the NCO in charge on a weekly schedule). Beginners began learning to drive on the jeep at the Elementary Driving School and were confined to the area of the motor pool. Upon graduation to Service Driving School they received instruction on the 4WD gravel truck and practised on the parade square. When a sufficient level of skill was reached, the fishermen students were allowed to drive to the antennae and back along the two-mile road. This trip was termed the cross-country, or point-to-point, and was much in demand by the students. None of the lessons were given freely. However, as before, fish were always acceptable as a form of currency.

The Caterpillar tractor was leased, once in a while, to a logging company in a nearby inlet. This lease was not as satisfactory as originally planned due to the monthly expense of renting a barge and tug to bring the tractor back to base for CO's inspection. On a couple of occasions this had to be done on *very* short notice.

Eventually, it was Insect Island's turn to be closed down permanently. The two Corporals were posted away, and the base was allowed to go unprotected after the hardware was removed. It was then more or less completely vandalized even before being stripped by the wreckers.

I lost touch with the Corporals. But somehow I believe they went on to greater fame and fortune.

* * *

It's difficult to give a true picture of the three temporary buildings that housed Air Force Headquarters for nearly forty years. But anyone who toiled in those alternately frigid or suffocating wooden structures – as I did in the early fifties – is not liable to forget them.

The main memory is one of dirt. It covered everything from the brindle-shit linoleum on the floors to the dust-laden venetian blinds on the filthy windows. The oak desks and straight-backed oak chairs were standard issue in each office. Only a hasty check of the walls for favourite photos or calendars assured anyone that they were in their rightful place.

The buildings were named A, B, and C. Perhaps letters were chosen over names because names would have been unprintable. All three buildings were connected by miles of halls, and it was easy to lose one's direction. Across the street lay the Elgin Hotel, and this was named E building. Both the army and the navy had foolishly located their Headquarters there, and the Defence Research Board had been enticed to occupy some back rooms.

The offices of the more senior types could be located in two ways. From the outside of the buildings an air conditioner poking from a window signified that a very senior type lurked inside. A man able to work right through an Ottawa August afternoon while the rest of the troops were stood down. From the interior of the buildings you could pick out the anointed by the green felt doors leading from the corridors into their sanctuaries. They were actually double doors, designed to conceal any wayward whispers.

In all the years I worked in those buildings I never heard or saw anything that could properly be called a secret. Admittedly, I wasn't a very senior type – but I did have access to most files. They were all, as one officer commented, "about as secret as a fart in a phone booth."

One of the interesting things about some of the offices was a strange phenomenon that eliminated buying a radio. The steam radiators were tuned to CFRA, a local radio station. Of course, you had to put your ear close to dirt-encrusted iron to get the news.

At one time – in order to check if indeed there was a night-cleaning staff – I nailed a fish under my boss's desk. I removed the shallow centre drawer, tacked the fish directly beneath the centre, and then refitted the drawer.

In about a week's time we discovered two things. The cleaning staff did come in at night: they began leaving nasty notes about the stench of fish. And the office windows could be pried open: our boss had to work that way for a week in the middle of winter.

The Headquarters went by various names: "The Poor Man's Pentagon," "The Kremlin," and "The Head Shed." Adding to their general greyness was the official order stating that all officers must wear civilian clothes, except for one day a month. This was designed to conceal from the population at large the true number of military types on the tax rolls.

Located deep in the dingy bowels of each building was a dark and dank canteen that stewed coffee and hot dogs and dispensed cardboard sandwiches. The canteen in A building was reported to be the best, but nobody ever proved why. Each morning, long queues of secretaries and erks snaked along the subterranean corridors leading to one of the three canteens. They were no larger than mobile chip-wagons and only catered to take-out orders. But they held an absolute monopoly since brewing your own coffee in your own office was taboo. The Camp Commandant spent most of his

ray tracy 35

time searching for illicit brewers. Evidently, the temporary buildings also had temporary electrical wiring. Too many coffee pots or hotplates sizzled it all.

Life was so dreary in those stuffy buildings that anything which challenged the boredom served as humour. One morning I decided to break our office routine – a long-existing office routine – which consisted of our boss ordering a coffee and a hot dog for his morning break. On that morning I volunteered to take the secretary's place and visit the canteen. I knew what the order would be, for I had heard it seven million times. I was prepared when he produced two thin dimes and announced that he wished a hot dog and coffee. Along with the dimes I got an admonition to ensure that the hot dog received a heavy coat of mustard.

When I repaired to the canteen I was armed with a condom and a pair of scissors. I removed the hot dog from its bun and slipped it inside the condom, drawing the condom up tight and cutting off the surplus with the scissors. Then I ladled on the mustard as directed.

When the boss took his first bite of that hot dog, clamping down on it with his front teeth, the condom stretched way out before it finally snapped back, splattering him with mustard. Unsure of what was happening he tried biting it again. And again he got showered with mustard. As we all howled with laughter he said, "If I didn't know better I'd say there was a safe on this hot dog!" When we told him to take another look, the hot dog – mustard, safe, and all – was hurled to the floor. It was too bad we couldn't have left the mess for the cleaners. That night they would have *had* to do some work.

*   *   *

Early in 1953, RCAF Station Penhold, Alberta, began its postwar life as No. 4 Service Flying Training School – and almost immediately a friendly rivalry developed with our sister station to the south at Claresholm. For some reason, Air Force Day was held in the fall that year. At least it was at those two stations. On the Friday before the big public event, our Commanding Officer received a message asking him to meet and pick up a parcel from a Claresholm aircraft which would fly into Penhold at 0700 hours the next morning.

Our CO was there on time to see a C-45 Expeditor aircraft land and taxi up. A crewman jumped out to hand the CO a parcel. Then he climbed back aboard and the aircraft taxied out and took off. Curious, our CO opened the parcel when he got back to his staff car parked on the flight line. He was mystified to find several lengths of wood, each about four feet long, and each with the pointed end of a nail sticking out one end. But he wasn't long left in doubt about their purpose. As he sat there, a gaggle of Harvards from Claresholm made a low pass down the flight line, dumping out paper as they passed over.

Upon examination, each paper exhorted the reader to visit Claresholm on Air Force Day!

Closing the Hangar Doors

London air raid shelters always provided the strangest encounters, but the happiest one for me occurred in the summer of 1943. Jamming into the shelter one night I suddenly confronted three fellows from Montreal who had been members of my senior class at high school.

They were all stationed at various air force bases in the north of England and they had planned things so they could spend their leave together. In short order I enlisted a Red Cross pal, also a former class mate – and since one of the guys had his English girl-friend with him, things paired out nicely. For two weeks we spent every evening dancing and whooping it up. It was just like old times back home – only better.

Shortly after this brief reunion two of the boys were shipped to the Middle East, where one was later killed. I have always cherished the memory of that happy interlude we shared in wartime London.

*　*　*

In 1941, our draft of air gunners arrived overseas at Stranraer. We were loaded aboard a train that made a swift, non-stop, all-night run to London.

We were all as green as grass, and when the train finally came to a squealing halt we had no idea where we might be. One of the air gunners opened a blackout curtain and peeked into the darkness. "Where are we, Mac?" someone asked him.

"We're at some bombed-out joint called St. Panacea," he said, misreading the station sign.

*　*　*

After our third day in England, at West Kirby outside Liverpool, the Commanding Officer called a best-blues, compulsory parade for all Canadians in camp. We were advised over the PA system to make it an all-out effort – shiny shoes, clean shaves, polished brass – the works.

After the usual BS that goes on at parades, and just before dismissal, the CO said that every airman from Toronto was to remain on the parade square. *What was this?* Immediately, we figured that it was a new way to get volunteers for the usual joe-jobs. But, after some hesitation, I decided to admit that I was from Toronto, and I remained behind with about fifty other airmen.

The group was formed up in ranks and once again given a thorough inspection. This inspection left about twenty-five of us. The others were dismissed. Then the CO got confidential and told us that we were to attend a dinner in Liverpool Town Hall the following day. It seemed that Toronto had adopted Liverpool during the blitz, and was sending food, blankets, medicines, and other necessities to help during those dark days. The dinner was a gesture of appreciation.

Vincent Massey, our Canadian High Commissioner, was the key-note speaker that evening. As we entered the Hall, each airman was taken in tow by one of the city fathers and his wife – and we dined that way, three to a table. Films were shown of the German bombings, and how the aid from Toronto was being used. We had speeches from the Lord Mayor and countless others. It was quite a high-toned affair.

Partway through our dinner I noticed that the lady at our table was extremely intent on the way I was eating. When our eyes met she asked, "Do all Canadians eat that way?"

I glanced around the Hall and noticed that – yes, indeed – all Canadians ate that way. Shovelling their food into their mouths with the fork held in the right hand.

"We are taught that it is very poor manners to eat with the right hand," she explained.

It was only then that I saw that the English were holding their forks in their left hand while they used their knives to push the food onto the back of the fork. They never put down either instrument.

The husband of the lady was extremely embarrassed and flustered. He hummed and stammered and finally said, "I think it's very poor manners on your part, my dear, to make an issue of it."

Needless to say, the rest of the meal proceeded in dead silence. But I remembered the lesson; and any time after that when I was eating with the English I used the fork in their style. I never had another embarrassing moment.

* * *

On the isolated stations during wartime you had to make your own fun or go bonkers. We had a Sergeant who came from New Brunswick somewhere, and he worked in Works and Buildings. He was a carpenter, I think. Anyhow, he would amble into our administrative building carrying one of those long spikes used for cleaning up paper and trash from lawns. Coming into our offices, he'd root around in our waste-baskets with his stick. He'd be mumbling, "That's not it . . . that's not it . . ." When someone would ask what he was looking for, the stock answer was: "My posting!"

* * *

Mart Kenny and his band played most of the air force stations during the war, and there was always a big turnout for the dance. Kenny would ask if there was anyone who would like to lead the band, and inevitably a few guys would get up to give it a try. The musicians would exaggerate their playing – which made for some queer-sounding music – and the crowd would give the airman conductor a rough time. But it was always good for a laugh.

* * *

During the war I was posted to Summerside, Prince Edward Island, but I couldn't get across to the island because the ferry had been damaged by ice in the strait. I holed up in Moncton to wait it out with some other NCO's – two in particular. One of them I considered a Nerd; but the other I really liked. He was a Warrant Officer pilot, and when the ferry service resumed and we went off to Summerside, I made sure that I got to room with him. We were quartered two to a room.

The Warrant Officer pilot was a nice guy – but I discovered that he had a problem. When I found him depressed one day and asked what had happened, he said that he had just received a severe reprimand from the Commanding Officer.

"What for?" I asked.

"Simply because I raised the wheels instead of the flaps," he said.

They made him a permanent Link Trainer instructor, and from then on he spent every night in the Sergeants' Mess trying to become an alcoholic. What I really detested was the lights snapping on at two in the morning as a couple of pals carried him into our room and threw him on his bed.

One day I had my best uniform cleaned and pressed – all ready

263

for the weekend and a two-day pass. When the time came to get dressed I couldn't find it anywhere. It turned out that my roomy had donned it and sashayed off to Charlottetown. It didn't matter to him that he had demoted himself to Sergeant, and exchanged his pilot's Wings for a wireless badge.

When he arrived back he was upset that I had moved across the hall and in with the Nerd. Who turned out to be one of the nicest guys I met in the service.

*　*　*

Near the end of the war, I was serving as an acting, unpaid Squadron Leader at a Service Flying Training School in western Ontario. On occasion, I had to mete out summary punishment to wayward trainees, and I heard a lot of stories – some interesting, some rather unimaginative. The best was delivered by a young Australian pilot trainee.

The culprit was a Royal Australian Air Force lad who, with a couple of his cobber friends, had been drinking beer in the Wets. He had pinched the Orderly Sergeant's motor transport, and he and his pals had crashed the barrier at the guard house and headed for the bright lights.

They were caught by the Service Police, returned to the station, and thrown in the digger until morning. Then they were brought to the Commanding Officer's Orderly Room. Marching in the leader, the Flight Sergeant stood him at attention in front of me and yelled at the top of his voice: "LAC Gray, David, on a charge, attention, sir!"

I said: "Number, rank, and name."

Out of the Aussie's mouth came something that sounded like this: "Five-Five-Oh-Nine-Ite; R-Eye-Eye-F; L-Eye-C; Dive Grigh."

"What have you been up to, Gray?" I asked.

"Well, mite, me and me oppos had a few pints, pinched the bloody van, and pissed off to town."

"Oh, and why was that?"

"Well, mite, I sigh, I ihn't doin' too well in me flyin' trynin' and ground school's a right bind so you might sigh I'd had the bloody biscuit."

Here the Flight Sergeant broke in with, "Say 'sir' when addressing the officer, Grigh – I mean Gray – and stop the bloody swearing."

I took the bull by the horns. "L-Eye-C Grigh," I said, "I'm givin' you five dighs in the bloody slammer, stoppin' your pie for five dighs, and confinin' your cobbers to camp for the same period. March him off, Flight."

The Flight Sergeant, not to be outdone, yelled: "Right, Grigh! Right turn, quick march!" Then he saluted me and, before he closed the office door, said, "Good show, mite! That's what I call stonin' the bloody crows!"

* * *

When we were stationed at No. 8 Bombing and Gunnery School at Lethbridge, we had several courses of Australian and New Zealand aircrew students. Everything about Canada was brand new to them, and they were delighted to take part in all activities. Whether it was hoisting a pair of girls' bloomers up the flagpole, or winning the beer drinking contests, those "down under" guys were front and centre.

Even though they detested the cold and snow, they seemed to get a particular thrill from watching the hockey games played on the outdoor rink. None of them had ever seen a hockey game and, of course, none had ever tried ice skating. It wasn't long before they determined that since it looked so easy they, too, would play a game – and after some discussion they decided it would be New Zealand vs. Australia.

On the day of the match the rink was lined with hundreds of cheering airwomen and airmen, all eager to witness a game that was the talk of the station. The crowd went wild as the ice began to be littered with sliding, toppling bodies. Some players made desperate efforts to keep upright by using their hockey sticks, while others tried to run on the sides of their skates as they held onto the boards. Some sat down and attempted to move forward with a rowing motion, while others crawled along on their hands and knees. Whenever a player got upright and made a quick dash forward, his skates would suddenly end up higher than his head. They were all covered with snow, but whether they were rolling on the ice or crashing over their mates – they still kept after that puck!

No goals were scored and it was a very short hockey game. But it was the funniest I have ever seen.

* * *

When I was stationed at Moncton, our baseball team journeyed down to Dorchester to play a game against the Dorchester Prison team. It was a good ballgame.

After it was over, an inmate came up to me and asked, "Did you let that bum of a pitcher strike you out?" I allowed that, yes, I guess he had – and the prisoner looked me over. "My name is Roberts, like yours," he informed me. "You know, you've disgraced the name Roberts!"

The other comment I remember took place when the game was in progress. A convict in the stands yelled out: "You guys better smarten up or it'll reflect on your R-211's!" Obviously, he had to be ex-RCAF. The R-211 was the air force promotion form.

* * *

No. I Manning Depot was located in the Canadian National Exhibition grounds on the Toronto lakeshore. It was only a short distance from the old baseball stadium, home of the Toronto Maple Leafs of the International League.

During the war years, the opening game of the season was cause for excitement each April. The RCAF was expected to mount a guard of honour. When the 1941 season opened, Billy Bishop (Air Marshal W.A. Bishop, VC) was asked to throw out the first ball.

Naturally, the whole camp wanted to get off duty and attend the game – and the excuses for leave passes went beyond the wildest imagination. Everyone had relatives who were dead or dying. I was kept busy all week refusing the most compassionate cases.

Just before closing the office on the Friday before the game, an airman requested permission to be paraded before me. I suspected what was coming before I agreed to see him.

The Sergeant marched in the sharpest looking airman I had ever seen. His uniform was absolutely immaculate. His shoes could have been mirrors, his buttons shone, his hair glistened. I had rarely, if ever, seen an airman turned out in such magnificent splendour.

When I asked his problem, he said: "Sir, I am a Toronto boy and my Dad has always taken me to the opening baseball game. I have an airman to take my place on duty. May I have a pass?"

I replied: "I'm happy to have an honest man in my squadron. Permission granted – but please tell your friends it's too late for them to change their stories."

* * *

In 1942, as a sprog Sergeant wireless technician, I was posted to Rivers, Manitoba, and given charge of a group of tradesmen. I was twenty-one years old and had never held a supervisory position.

Our task, I was told, was to build DRT's at all Air Observer Schools and Operational Training Units across Canada. A DRT was something brand new – in fact one hadn't been built before. The initials stood for Dead Reckoning Trainer.

My direct supervisor was located at Air Force Headquarters in Ottawa. We would be on temporary duty, it turned out, for three years. No one ever seemed to know where we were or where we were supposed to be or what we were doing. And it seemed that no one cared. We got to see our supervisor every six months or so, and then only for a very brief time.

My immediate interest lay in the tradesmen I was suddenly responsible for. They were all a lot older than I was and many were double my age. I had three electricians, three wireless techs, and three carpenters. It was the carpenters who stood out and wrote themselves large on my memory. One was from Cape Breton, and had been a casket maker before the war. A guy of about fifty, he was, I discovered, an alcoholic. The second was a farmer from Ontario, and the third had worked in the bush. These were the initial three – there were others as the years rolled along.

It was, of course, wartime – and anyone claiming to have a skill of any kind was immediately hired. This gave rise to many jokes about these "skilled" tradesmen. One concerned a carpenter, newly-hired, who was busy pounding nails into a wall of a temporary building. His foreman noticed that he was throwing half the nails on the ground. When questioned as to why he was doing this, he said, "Some of the nails have the heads on the wrong end." To which the foreman reportedly replied, "You fool! Those are for the other side of the wall."

On our first assignment we were sent out to the OTU at Pat Bay in British Columbia, but on the RAF side of the base. There we reported to an officer in the Ground Instruction School for further orders. We had to purchase our materials locally, and it took some time to round up the two-by-fours, plywood, and lumber that we needed. Finally, we began to erect the shell of the building, and in the first few days we made great progress.

We were all banging away with our hammers, sawing and trimming, when I was challenged by an RAF officer. He accused me of not telling him that a further number of carpenters had been assigned to the station. I was completely confused by his allegation. Then it dawned on me. All of us were helping in the work – it hadn't occurred to us not to – so the RAF type thought that we were *all* carpenters. But we didn't make any distinctions. When the carpenters weren't busy with hammers and saws they helped run the miles of wire we needed.

Well before we completed the trainer the carpenters ran out of work, and one day I was approached by an RAF officer who asked if one of them could build some shelves in his office. This seemed like a reasonable request to me, but when I approached a carpenter by the name of George about it, he replied: "Tell the officer to go fuck himself!" After some mental anguish I decided that since we were due to pull out in a couple of days I wouldn't pursue the matter. I needed George more than I needed the RAF officer and his shelves. But I could feel that I was on my way to a head of grey hair.

On the next station, there came a day when I couldn't find the carpenters. I searched everywhere on the base before I discovered that they had taken a contract in town to replace a local's roof. Then, when one of the carpenters who had gone on a two-day pass hadn't shown up after a week, I really began to worry. Surely, this time I would have to report him. When he finally arrived back I pounced on him. "Just where in the hell have you been?" I asked. He said that he had decided to get married and had gone on his honeymoon!

But the carpenters did come in handy when we arrived on a station, and – through the usual snafu – the materials we needed hadn't arrived or were unavailable. George, in particular, would shine. He knew that there was always a contractor on base who

270

was building something or other and had materials (just the ones we wanted) piled up somewhere . . . .

I will always remember George's whispered rallying cry as we crept along in the dark. "Foller me, lads, and I'll show yez the way."

* * *

One day a disreputable mutt invaded our base. After some days of searching every inch of the station, he chose the Officers' Mess for his official residence. This happened in the spring of 1945, and the dog's arrival coincided with a general face-lifting and cleanup of the station.

Our Commanding Officer blew a gasket when he discovered the dog, and ordered the hound taken out to the boon docks and disposed of. A fellow by the name of Nicholson was given this unsavoury task – but he didn't have the heart to shoot the dog. Instead, he drove it about ten miles into the country, hoping that it would be adopted. He was certain, anyway, that it would never find its way back.

About four days later the mutt limped into camp. He was all muddy and starving. The whole station was delighted to have him back, and since the CO was away on a conference, things went smoothly for a few days. In fact, the Sergeants were so impressed with the dog's survival and its obvious devotion to the RCAF that they quickly adopted him as their Mess mascot.

The Wing Commander had hardly returned to base when he ran across the dog and went into a rage. He threatened to put Nicholson on charge for dereliction of duty, refusing to believe that he had driven the dog out into the country. When the adjutant corroborated the story the CO had a change of heart and he, too, became impressed with the dog's devotion. He agreed to let the Sergeants keep their mascot – with the proviso that the dog must be kept free of fleas and bathed at least once a week.

From then on Saturday mornings became ablution time for the mutt, and you would see the NCO's chasing all over camp trying to capture him. He was a clever old dog and he hated being bathed. When bath-time approached he always took off, a yelling mob of Sergeants in pursuit.

The whole thing was pretty silly – but the dog eventually became a fixture around the camp. He had the complete run of the place. I remember one morning when a reconnaissance plane crash-landed on a field behind the airmen's barracks. The dog was first on the scene, and he raised such a rumpus that, for a moment, the crew were afraid to get out of their crashed aircraft.

*   *   *

Among my souvenirs from those long-departed days with No. 1 Group Headquarters in Newfoundland is the official photograph of our Administrative Section. That particular relic from those war years shows the happiest group of airmen and airwomen imaginable. We were absolutely in stitches when the shutter clicked.

We had been told to assemble – uniforms pressed and buttons shining – immediately after breakfast on a Sunday morning. At that hour, a good many of our NCO's had not recovered from their Saturday night bash in the Sergeants' Mess, and they had trouble meeting the deadline.

The photographer, tripod in place, had great difficulty in positioning everyone. Much to our amusement, he kept shifting people back and forth. Finally all was ready, and he stepped behind his camera. But then, at the last minute, he decided that it would look better if the seated front row crossed their ankles while the two Sergeants, who were at each end of the row, crossed their legs. These two Sergeants had barely made the roll call in time – but they now sat with buttons gleaming and shoes polished to a spit. They were dignity personified.

"Ready . . . everybody smile . . ." the photographer coaxed.

Then once again he jumped from behind his camera.

"No, no, no!" he cried, waving his hands and pointing to the Sergeants.

We all turned to look. Our two cross-legged, dignified NCO's were flashing several inches of naked ankle. They were banished to the back row and when the photographer again ordered, "A big smile everyone!" he had no trouble at all.

*   *   *

I went to work at age sixteen in the laundry room at the Royal York Hotel in Toronto. After working my way up to Room Clerk

at the hotel, I joined the RCAF for aircrew training in 1941. The first stop in my RCAF career was Manning Depot, where the Commanding Officer was a former North York Bible Class preacher who strutted around like a peacock in the mating season, all spit and polish. After a few nasty encounters we all learned to avoid The Preacher's path.

After navigation training I went overseas as a Sergeant navigator. I had hardly crewed up when our aircraft crashed and everyone else was killed. I kicked around with "odd bods" from other crashes, before being posted to No. 57 Squadron where I joined an all-Sergeant crew. I was the only Canadian – but we had a Newfie pilot (who was one hell of a man, one hell of a pilot, and hell on the ladies). During our tour we had four flight engineers. The first three went LMF, and for the last ten trips of our tour we never knew with whom we were going to fly.

I had completed my tour before I knew that I had been commissioned. Serving on an RAF squadron isolated you from the RCAF, and they had lost track of me. It wasn't until I inquired about getting paid that they told me I was an officer. The best part of my visit was receiving officer's back pay. It was back-dated to my first operation. The sad part of the visit was learning that I had been posted to Warrington for shipment back to Canada.

When I arrived at Warrington my officer's uniform (which I had ordered) had yet to catch up to me. I was straggling around in a half-RCAF and half-RAF battle-dress. Moreover, I hadn't put up the campaign ribbons which we were obliged to wear (and which few of us desired to wear). I was startled to find that – lo and behold – the CO of Warrington was none other than our old pal, The Preacher. This time he was strutting around wearing a side-arm, trying to imitate a Battle of Britain pilot. He immediately gave us all shit for our general appearance, our attitudes, and our sloppiness.

We were not, according to The Preacher, going to be accorded any privileges just because we had completed a tour of operations. We would, he proclaimed, in a Bible Class voice, "Shape up. Spruce up. And get our ribbons up, by God!"

We dissolute types all shuffled off parade muttering "Fuck you!" We really had no idea what decorations he was talking about. I decided that a visit to our Orderly Room might produce some answers.

A cute WAAF waited on me and she rhymed off three campaign medals I should have been wearing. I forget what she called them – but we called them the NAAFI, the Spam, and the Sally Anne. When I inquired about my wound stripe she checked her records but couldn't find anything recorded. I showed her a scar on my finger (which I got opening a can of chicken, sent overseas by my wife), and explained that it was the result of flak action over Germany. I told her it had happened when I stuck my finger out the window to check on the wind direction. She said that she would check further with records centre in London.

None of this seemed to please The Preacher very much, and I received a tongue lashing for being irreverent and facetious. It was a happy day when we sailed away from Warrington and home to Canada and civvy street . . . .

A year or so later I was back at the Royal York Hotel – but this time as Reservations Manager. During these early postwar years two things were as scarce as hens' teeth: hotel rooms and automobiles.

One day I received a telephone call from the proprietor of a large car dealership in Toronto. After a moment of disbelief, I realized that I was talking to The Preacher – and that he urgently wanted several rooms in my hotel! I was so incredibly delighted to hear his voice that I had great difficulty controlling my urge to interrupt him – until he suggested that, as the quid pro quo of his request, I could have a new car for only two hundred dollars over list price. Then, with the greatest of pleasure, I told him in no uncertain terms to "get stuffed."

* * *

The wartime myth said that women could never adjust to service life. They could never be friends, as men are friends, or develop the same kind of camaraderie.

How odd, then, to find that those wartime WD's still treasure the friendships started in basic training. How strange it is that, if they could not adjust, so many women lived together in such congested quarters. There was no squabbling. Not in any of the barracks I lived in.

I don't claim that everything was rosy. How could that be with such diversity? There were girls with different educational levels and different family backgrounds from different parts of Canada. There were girls who sometimes spoke different languages. All of us were quartered twenty or so to a room in which each of us had one bunk (upper or lower), a tiny locker, a shelf, and a length of rod for hanging uniforms. That was the extent of our privacy. The only time you were really alone was in the tub or shower. Everyone learned. Everyone adjusted. Whether they came from the city or, like me, from the farm.

I met people with great courage. Like the girl with a deformed back who took more abuse than anyone should have to take from a screaming drill Sergeant – until, one day, someone else in the flight yelled back at him in a fury, not caring what he might do. He did nothing and the abuse stopped.

I discovered how insensitive people can be. We watched a non-English-speaking girl trying to function in a room where there were only English-speaking girls – until, one day, she paraded naked through all the rooms. She vanished from the station and was never mentioned again. But I knew instinctively that there, but for some accident, went I.

I learned the rules and reasons for marking everything with name and serial number. And I learned to be cautious about leaving small items, like collars, in the laundry room – even if they were marked. No one remained gullible and trusting for very long.

In fact, service was a continual learning experience. I remember going to a dance on the station. As usual, there were more girls than boys, and if you liked to dance, as I did, you had to ask a guy and chance rejection, It was nerve-wracking. That evening I noticed a pleasant-looking man, just standing on the sidelines watching all the dancers. After some hesitation I summoned up my nerve and approached him. All around me the action seemed to stop. It was only after I had asked him to dance that I figured out what insignia he was wearing! He smiled and said something about how he liked to dance – but usually no one ever asked or expected it of a Padre.

I remember those things more vividly than the boring business of drills and lectures and polishing shoes (and buttons) and lining up for innoculation shots and scrubbing barracks floors for inspections . . . .

The promises that the air force made when I walked into that recruiting station in Saskatoon in 1942 – travel, flying, training in Intelligence work – never materialized. What I did get from the air force was something I never expected. An incomparable education in people, and a host of friends, unforgotten over all the years.

Printed in Canada